first names

MUSK

Tracey Turner

Illustrations by Mike Smith

For Toby, who is also full of bright ideas

First Names: ELON MUSK
is a
DAVID FICKLING BOOK

First published in Great Britain in 2018 by
David Fickling Books,
31 Beaumont Street,
Oxford, OX1 2NP

Text © Tracey Turner, 2018
Illustrations © Mike Smith, 2018

978-1-910989-62-3

1 3 5 7 9 10 8 6 4 2

The right of Tracey Turner and Mike Smith to be identified
as the author and illustrator of this work has been asserted
in accordance with the Copyright, Designs and Patents Act 1988.

Papers used by David Fickling Books are from well-managed
forests and other responsible sources.

Mixed Sources
Product group from well-managed
forests and other products

A CIP cata   Library.

Prin   c.

All the facts   and are
accurate to t   ou think
may be incorr   J338.4092 MUS JUNIOR   £6.99   rtaining,
that's why   ; the
words and th   rds and
thoughts of t   sometimes just for fun – and the
Elon Explains sections aren't explained in Elon Musk's own words.

names

Elon
MUSK

Who will you get to know next?

Coming soon ...

Contents

Introduction – Pretoria, South Africa, 1981   7

1 – Elon's Easter Eggs and Blasting Stars   10

2 – Elon Takes a Plane   29

3 – Elon Makes Millions   43

4 – Elon on Mars   57

5 – Elon Blasts Off   68

6 – Elon's Falcons and Dragons   87

7 – Elon's Electric Cars   102

8 – What Elon Did Next   121

Timeline   136

Glossary   138

Index   141

Introduction – Pretoria, South Africa, 1981

'Five...four...three...two...one...'

Everyone else was out and Elon had the back garden to himself. The fuse was lit. He and the cat were at a safe distance. The moment had arrived.

'...zero!'

With an impressive *whooosh!* the rocket whizzed into the air.

'We have lift off! Yes!'

The cat fled. Elon squinted into the cloudless sky, following the rocket's path. It soared way beyond the roof of the house, until it was just a speck up above him. Then the fuel ran out and it plummeted back to the ground, smashing into the patio.

This was his most impressive launch yet. The rocket had travelled up 50 metres or more, it hadn't exploded, and Elon and the cat were both unharmed. What a result.

'Right,' said Elon, gathering up the broken bits of rocket. 'I'm going to make an even better one.'

As we're about to find out, Elon's childhood passion for rocket-building never left him. He did make an even better rocket – in fact, he's now making **the most powerful space rocket in the whole world**.

But before we follow Elon's rockets into orbit, let's find out a bit more about him.

This is Elon Musk today

 Hi!

He looks like a pretty ordinary kind of guy, but beneath that cool exterior lurks a brain the size of a planet. He's an expert on rocket science, has a new and revolutionary idea about once a week, and never forgets a fact. He's an entrepreneur engineer and inventor who's sent mice into orbit, built awesome electric cars, inspired a mega-successful movie, and become one of the world's richest people.

The money really isn't all that important.

But what about the supercars and the mansions?

I've found much more interesting ways to spend my cash.

Elon does have a point there. He's used his own money to fund the super-powerful spacecraft he's developing. Another of the amazing things he's doing is a mind-blowing mission to **save the human**

race from extinction – by helping us become a multiplanetary species, starting with a colony on Mars.

But Elon wouldn't be building the biggest space rockets in the world without single-minded determination and total belief in what he's doing. Before his incredible success, he had to cope with a good deal of failure.

> Exploding rockets, that sort of thing. But you have to take a few risks in life.

Maybe you have your own ambitions for saving humanity or changing the world for ever. If so, or even if you just like the sound of the rockets, the fast cars and the space mice, you are definitely going to be interested in Elon's story. There's a space greenhouse in here as well, and lots of video games. Oh, and Justin Bieber turns up at one point . . .

> Get on with it!

Exactly! What are you waiting for? Turn the page to find out all about the incredible life of the awesome Elon Musk.

1 Elon's Easter Eggs and Blasting Stars

So, how does a rocket-building, Mars-colonizing billionaire start off in life? In Elon's case (and, to be honest, he's just about the only rocket-building, Mars-colonizing billionaire out there), he lived with his family in Pretoria, South Africa. Was he a boy genius who was full of money-making ideas and amazed everyone with his scientific knowledge? Yes, of course he was. But let's start at the beginning.

Elon was born in 1971, and back then South Africa could be a tough place to grow up. The government separated people of different races – children even had to go to different schools – and black people didn't have the same rights as white people. Things were extremely unfair, and often a little tense, to say the least. On the other hand, the Musks were well off. They didn't own a private jet or anything flash like that, but Errol Musk, Elon's dad, was a successful engineer, and Maye Musk, his mum, was a nutritionist and model.

You might want to take a moment to get your head around the full horror of this next bit, because – even though they could easily have afforded it – **Mr and Mrs Musk didn't give their children any**

pocket money! How on earth did Elon and his younger brother and sister – Kimbal and Tosca (the family liked interesting names) – get their hands on unhealthy snacks, toys and comics?

Two of Elon's younger cousins had similar pocket-money problems. They lived close by – their mum and Elon's mum were twin sisters – and when Elon came up with some brilliant plans, they were keen to get involved. Despite the unimaginable horror of not having any pocket money, the children were allowed plenty of freedom to do what they wanted and so some of those plans actually succeeded. Here's one of the best:

An Eggstreme Solution

By the time Elon was around 15, he'd already had a lot of practice finding solutions to the pocket-money problem, and now he turned his attention to chocolate. He couldn't help noticing that Easter eggs were expensive, but chocolate bars were cheap, so he put a business idea to Kimbal and his cousins:

The cousins took their Easter eggs around the wealthiest streets in Pretoria, and used a clever sales pitch to sell them for about ten times the going rate.

It worked! The cousins made a tidy sum.

If you were just off to buy some cheap chocolate and silver foil, stop right there. Easter eggs are much cheaper now so this clever scheme wouldn't work today.

Adventurous Oldsters

Elon and his cousins were certainly an adventurous bunch, and that might have had something to do with their grandparents, Joshua and Wyn Haldeman. Sadly, grandad Joshua died when Elon was only three, but granny Wyn lived on to tell the children about their many daring adventures. She even gave slide shows to prove her stories were true. Among other things, the two oldsters . . .

- Flew a single-engine plane all over Canada, with their kids in the back.

- Moved to South Africa and became the first people ever to fly a single-engine plane from there to Australia – a whopping 30,000 miles!

- Came joint first, beating professional drivers, in a 12,000-kilometre car race through Africa.

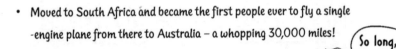

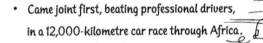

- Searched for the fabled Lost City of the Kalahari Desert, which meant the whole family camping in the African bush with hungry hyenas, leopards and lions circling. Wyn had to patrol the perimeter with her rifle.

Meet the Family

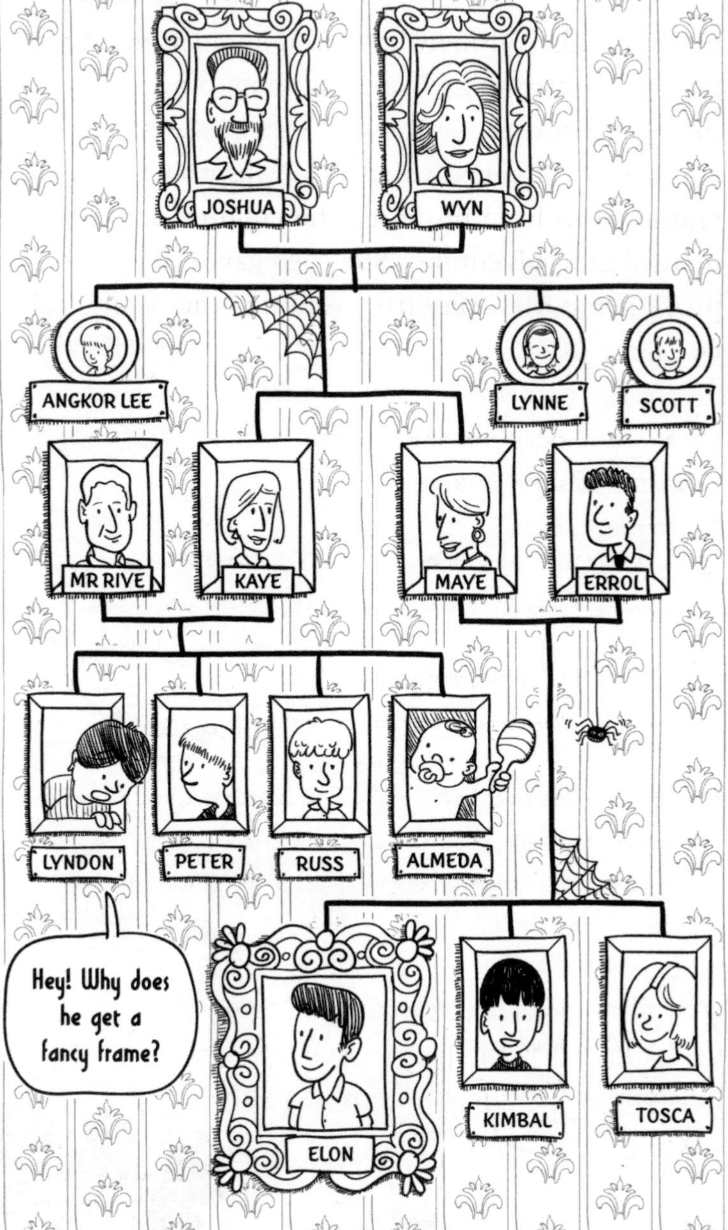

Superheroes and Explosions

Elon absolutely loved a good adventure story, whether it was true or made up, and he soon discovered the wonderful world of reading. He was mad about comic books like *Superman*, *Batman*, *Spider-man* and *Green Lantern*, and science fiction and fantasy novels too. One of his all-time favourite books was *The Hitchhiker's Guide to the Galaxy* by Douglas Adams, partly because it taught him that asking the right question makes it easier to find the right answer, but also because it's brilliantly funny and has some of the best aliens ever.

If you've ever spent a whole afternoon with your nose in a book, you're in good company – reading was one of Elon's favourite hobbies. Some days he **read for a solid ten hours**.

In fact he liked reading so much that before long he'd finished all the fiction books in the school library.

He went to the local public library and finished all the fiction there as well. After that he turned to non-fiction.

He soon realized there was an awful lot of stuff he didn't know, and set about putting that right as quickly as he could. With no internet, he worked his way through massive encylopaedias that covered every subject under the Sun and, having an **amazing memory**, he soon had loads of fascinating facts at his fingertips. The family found that asking Elon was much quicker than looking things up for themselves.

Elon found science really exciting, and, as we've already seen, he especially liked rockets – he was fascinated by the speed they could travel and the explosive fuel they used. Having

a fair bit of time on his hands, and without any pesky adults around, he started making and testing out rockets he designed himself. Obviously, this **was extremely dangerous** – so definitely don't try it at home (or anywhere else for that matter). Most dangerous of all was the rocket fuel that Elon concocted – he experimented with different chemicals **causing several loud explosions**.

BOOM!

Blast off!

When Elon gets interested in something, he tends to stick with it, so nearly blowing up his own home didn't put him off. Soon he was dreaming of becoming an astronaut and travelling in a much bigger space rocket (one that didn't explode).

Tough Times and First Love

Despite Elon's comfortable life, with holidays abroad and stuff like that, things weren't always happy at home.

> Our trip to the United States was totally awesome!

Elon's mum and dad got divorced when Elon was nine years old. His mum took the three children to live in Durban, more than 600 kilometres away, while his dad stayed in Pretoria. Elon must have found that hard, because after a couple of years he decided to move back to his dad's. Later Kimbal moved back too, but the family was still divided and everyone was unhappy about that.

However, Elon had found something to distract him: **he had fallen in love**. But it wasn't *that* sort of love affair . . .

Elon saw a computer for sale in an electronics shop in Johannesburg and fell head over heels. He loved reading and he loved science, but he was properly in love with computers. When Elon was born, computers were big and clunky and not very powerful. But by the 1980s some were actually small enough to sit on a desk and cheap enough for people to buy and have in their own homes.

This new technology well and truly blew Elon's mind and he pestered his dad until he got a PC of his own. It came with a manual for a programming language called BASIC, which Elon managed to master **in three days flat**. That included the nights – Elon couldn't rest until he'd cracked it. This was probably some sort of record because, for ordinary humans, BASIC is supposed to take about six months to learn!

Blasting Stars

Then, of course, there were computer games. They didn't have the fancy graphics we have today, but they were still a lot of fun. Now that Elon had learned computer programming, he didn't see why he couldn't create his own game, and you won't be surprised to learn that that's exactly what he did.

Elon's game was called Blastar. It was a shooting game set in space (blast star – see what he did there?).

Players had to destroy an alien spacecraft carrying hydrogen bombs and 'status beam machines' (whatever they are). For a 12-year-old, that in itself was no mean achievement, but there was more. Calling himself E. R. Musk (because he thought it was the sort of name a science fiction writer might have), Elon actually managed to sell the code for the game to a computer magazine. It was the first time he really showed off his phenomenal business skills, and **he made a tidy $500** – now *that* was serious pocket money.

Space rockets and million-dollar software companies were just around the corner.

Elon Introduces the Latest Technology

Today a basic laptop has around 800,000 times the memory of Elon's PC, but back in the '80s having a PC in your own home was absolutely amazing.

Hardly anyone had heard of the internet back then and being able to record and watch a movie at home seemed incredibly exciting.

All the best games were in the arcades. The machines there wouldn't fit inside your home.

80s technology is absolutely awesome, and in the future it's just going to get better and better!

Elon's Arcade

Picture the scene: it's the 1980s and you're obsessed with video games. Do you:

a) Spend all your spare time in a video arcade

b) Go into business and open a video arcade yourself

c) Do both of the above?

You can probably guess what Elon and his brother, sister and cousins did. After all, they were the perfect team, with their expert knowledge of the best games available. They didn't think twice about finding a shop, renting it and **ordering some enormous games machines** (the size of a sofa).

They were all set to make a fortune when disaster struck: it turned out they needed permission from the local council to go into business, and to get it at least one of them had to be eighteen years old. Elon was the oldest, but he was still only sixteen. The cousins hadn't told their parents what they were up to – in case they interfered – and when the kids were forced to ask for help, the grown-ups did not go along with the plan . . .

The arcade never opened.

Grim School Days

Away from his family, school life for Elon was grim. He was super brainy, but small for his age and not very good at sport. Unfortunately, being big, tough and sporty helped kids to win friends at Elon's school, but being brainy didn't. Plus, Elon was a bit different from most of the other kids.

Poor Elon was picked on and bullied. He tried minding his own business, but that didn't keep him away from trouble. One day he was sitting innocently eating his packed lunch at the top of some stone steps when . . .

Elon ended up **unconscious** and had to stay in hospital for a week. You'd think the children who'd attacked him would have been expelled from school and flung into prison or something, but, unbelievably, **they weren't even punished**. The school said it was just schoolboy high spirits. The teachers seemed to think bullying was part of growing up and that kids should learn to get on with it – they wouldn't get away with that today.

Bill Gates, the mega-successful founder of Microsoft, once said:

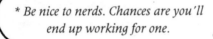

* Be nice to nerds. Chances are you'll end up working for one.

* This is an actual quote.

The bullies probably never imagined that one day someone as brilliant, clever and important as Bill Gates would become Elon's friend. And, sadly, his wise advice came too late.

Elon went to a different school once he'd recovered, and things were better there, but the injuries to his nose left him with permanent breathing problems – a painful reminder of his grimmest time at school.

Despite his amazing brain, Elon wasn't always top of the class. He got excellent marks in the subjects he liked, but wasn't too bothered about the ones he didn't. He'd get really fired up about some things – for instance he argued passionately in favour of solar energy in a science debate, but he was **way ahead of his time** and the rest of the class thought he was talking rubbish. Why bother with new-fangled ideas involving the Sun when you could dig up coal, oil and gas instead?

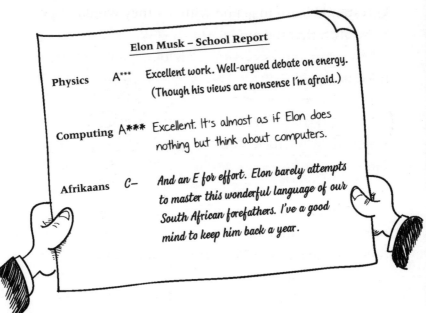

Elon Musk – School Report

Physics	A***	Excellent work. Well-argued debate on energy. (Though his views are nonsense I'm afraid.)
Computing	A***	Excellent. It's almost as if Elon does nothing but think about computers.
Afrikaans	C–	And an E for effort. Elon barely attempts to master this wonderful language of our South African forefathers. I've a good mind to keep him back a year.

Avoiding the Army

You might expect that Elon couldn't wait to finish school, but in South Africa in the 1980s school leavers had something absolutely awful to look forward to

– military service. At the age of eighteen, all white men had to join the South African army for two years, and one of the army's main jobs was to make sure everyone stuck to the government's horrible, racist rules.

Elon definitely did not want to join up, so when he was seventeen, before he found himself in uniform saluting a sergeant major, he started to think of a way out. He was still in love with computers, so where better to head than America, where most of the supercool new technology was coming from? His mum was originally from Canada – which, you might have noticed, is right next to America – so that seemed like a good place to start. Elon's adventures were about to begin.

2 Elon Takes a Plane

Elon had a vague plan to stay with his great uncle in Montreal, Canada, but he didn't do anything sensible like checking exactly where his great uncle lived and whether he had a spare room. Instead, he jumped on a plane, travelled a whopping 13,000 kilometres across the world, and *then* tried to find his uncle by looking up his number and calling from a pay phone. Unfortunately for Elon, **his great uncle wasn't in**.

In fact, Elon's great uncle wasn't even in Canada. He was in Minnesota, over the border in the United States and 1,800 kilometres away! So Elon spent his first night in Canada on his own in a youth hostel.

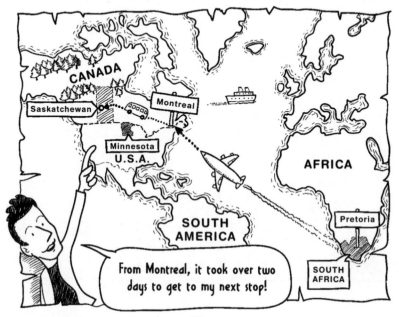

From Montreal, it took over two days to get to my next stop!

Log Chopping and Gloop Shovelling

Elon didn't mess about. He quickly bought a roving bus ticket and travelled to Saskatchewan, a huge prairie province in the middle of Canada, which is a full 3,000 kilometres away from Montreal. His grandparents had lived in Saskatchewan and it was where his mum had grown up. He still had a cousin there, in fact, and the cousin happened to be home. Elon arrived in time to celebrate his own eighteenth birthday and stayed for a while, to help out on his cousin's farm.

As he travelled around Canada, meeting relatives and making new friends, Elon paid his way by chainsawing logs (there's a lot of log-chopping in Canada because the country has zillions of trees). He wasn't afraid of hard work, and some of it was very hard indeed. Elon's worst and most dangerous job was cleaning out the boiler room in a lumber yard.

You just crawl through there . . .

10 minutes later

Another 15 minutes later

31

Could you have stuck it? Out of 30 people who started the job, **only three had the strength and willpower to last more than a week** – and Elon was one of them. Gloop shovelling was the best-paid job Elon could get, so he must have thought the heat, the smell and the life-threatening conditions were worth it. But as he shovelled, he was almost certainly planning easier ways of making a living.

Two Universities (and Some Romance)

After all that shovelling and chainsawing and travelling about, going to study at Queen's University in Kingston, Ontario must have felt like a relaxing holiday. For Elon, university was way better than school. He was able to study just the subjects that interested him and he made some good friends too, who actually liked the fact that he was brainy and didn't think his ideas were daft. Elon even fell in love again, and this time it wasn't with a computer. Justine Wilson was the coolest girl on campus (according to Elon) and superbrainy too. She wasn't quite so crazy about him at first, but eventually . . .

When Elon wasn't studying, or spending time with Justine, he sold computers and computer parts, or fixed and built PCs for the other students, who quickly discovered he was absolutely brilliant at it. Elon did it mainly because he still really loved computers, but it was also a great way to make some cash.

After two years at Queen's, Elon won a scholarship to the University of Pennsylvania (Penn for short), to study economics and physics. He was only 20, but he had done it: **he was finally going to live in the United States, just as he'd planned**. And he was going to one of the best universities in the country.

As you can imagine, Elon began impressing tutors and fellow students at Penn straight away. Ever since his **heated** debate in secondary school, he'd had a **burning** interest in solar energy and he spent an awful lot of time thinking about it . . .

Why? Because it's sun-sational!

Solar Energy and Fossil Fuels

We humans guzzle an awful lot of energy and most of it comes from fossil fuels . . .

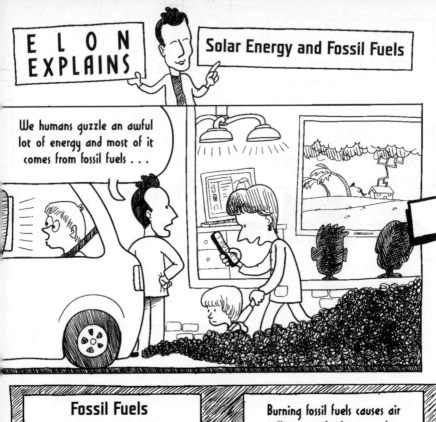

Fossil Fuels

Fossil fuels come from energy made by plants and animals that lived millions of years ago. All living things contain lots of carbon.

Burning fossil fuels causes air pollution and releases carbon dioxide into the atmosphere. This traps more heat and makes Earth warmer.

Yikes!

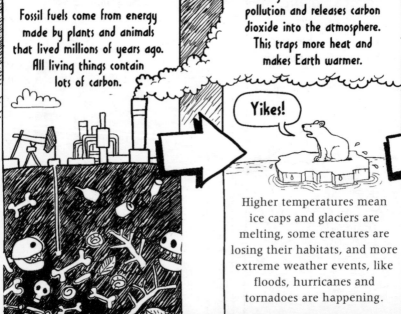

Higher temperatures mean ice caps and glaciers are melting, some creatures are losing their habitats, and more extreme weather events, like floods, hurricanes and tornadoes are happening.

... which is stupid — it's like some crazy experiment to see how bad things can get!

Cough!

Splutter!

We haven't had this much carbon dioxide in the atmosphere for millions of years — back when apes started to walk on two legs.

Fossil fuels are going to run out some day. But you might have noticed ...

... there's this fireball in the sky that turns up every day and provides more than enough energy to keep us all warm, fuel our cars and everything. So, why aren't we using it? Are we mad?

Solar panels contain photovoltaic cells which turn sunlight into electricity

Power from solar panels doesn't cause pollution. And, just like wind power and other renewable sources of energy, it won't run out any time soon.
Thanks to Elon, you can even buy roof tiles that collect solar energy.

Elon came up with all sorts of brilliant ideas about new solar technology, including huge solar panels in space transmitting energy to Earth using microwave beams. He had ideas about other things too, like new ways to store energy, and massive databases a bit like the ones Google uses today. He was way ahead of his time.

Party Time at Penn!

It wasn't all hard work at university though . . .

At Penn, Elon and his friend, Adeo Ressi, rented a big house with TEN bedrooms. All week, they'd work hard (apart from the occasional gaming binge), then **at weekends, they'd party**. They transformed the house into disco central by sticking black plastic bags over the windows to block out the light and decorating the place with luminous paint. Up to 500 partygoers paid an entry fee, in exchange for drinks, music and bags of atmosphere. And with Elon in charge of the organization, they could make enough money in just one night to pay their rent for a whole month!

Despite being a quiet and fairly shy sort of person, Elon still **absolutely loves parties** today, and over the years he's come up with some extravagant party ideas. For his 30th birthday, he rented an English castle for 20 of his friends and family – they stayed up all night playing games like sardines and hide-and-seek. Another party involved an overnight trip on the Orient Express. He likes fancy dress too . . .

Holiday Time

The parties stopped in the summer holidays, though, and Elon went to work over on the west coast of America, in California's Silicon Valley.

Elon being Elon, he didn't just have one holiday job, he had two. By day, he researched fuel sources for electric vehicles and by night, he headed over to a company called Rocket Science Games and wrote code. It wasn't much of a holiday, but Elon loved it so much he worked in Silicon Valley two summers in a row.

By now, Elon's mum, sister and brother had moved to the US, and in 1994, at the end of the summer, Elon and Kimbal **set off on a road trip** from San Francisco. They both loved cars, so they spent some of their hard-earned cash on an old BMW, which they drove right across the United States, arriving at Penn for the start of the new term.

CANADA

SALT LAKE CITY

SAN FRANCISCO

OMAHA

CHICAGO

PHILADELPHIA

UNIVERSITY OF PENNSYLVANIA

MEXICO

The car was almost as old as they were and it kept overheating and breaking down, so the brothers sometimes had to drive with the heaters on full blast in sweltering weather to stop the engine from getting too hot. When they weren't busy fixing the car, they took turns driving and spent an awful lot of time talking. They'd planned pocket money schemes together as kids – now they were dreaming up ideas for a business they could start together.

A Big Question

Party (and study) time at Penn came to an end in 1995, and Elon had to think about what he wanted to do next.

Elon liked the idea of working in video games very much – just imagine doing your favourite things and getting paid for it! – but his future plans were much more ambitious than that. He wasn't just considering his own health, wealth and happiness – he'd actually been asking himself a seriously big question: **what's the most important thing of all?** And he'd started thinking about the future of everyone on the entire planet.

He realized that human beings were in terrible danger . . .

Elon could have tried to sort the world's pollution problem, or come up with an amazing invention to reverse climate change, but people were still going to run out of room one day – or the Earth might be hit by a giant asteroid. They needed somewhere else to go . . .

The solution was obvious – to Elon, anyway. And it involved rockets.

We need to find humanity a new planet to live on – and fast! We should be exploring space more!

But sending rockets to a distant planet was never going to be easy for a 24-year-old who'd just left college – plus there were a couple of other super-important things Elon wanted to get to grips with:

1. The internet – it was new and Elon understood, even then, that it was destined to change the whole world in the very near future. And . . .

2. Solar power – because fossil fuels were causing the climate to change, and they were going to run out anyway.

He wasn't absolutely sure what he should concentrate on first, but he was itching to get out there and sow the seeds for his ultimate mission . . .

. . . to **SAVE** humanity!

3 Elon Makes Millions

So, how do you become a space-exploring superhero? Is there an apprenticeship you can do, or maybe a special secret training camp or something? No, of course there isn't. Elon had to work it out for himself.

First he got himself a place at Stanford University in California to do a further degree in materials science and physics. But Silicon Valley was just down the road and after just two days **Elon changed his mind**. He decided that starting a new company with Kimbal would help save humanity faster and he left university for good.

I could do something mega-exciting, make lots of money and save humanity all at the same time!

Come back!

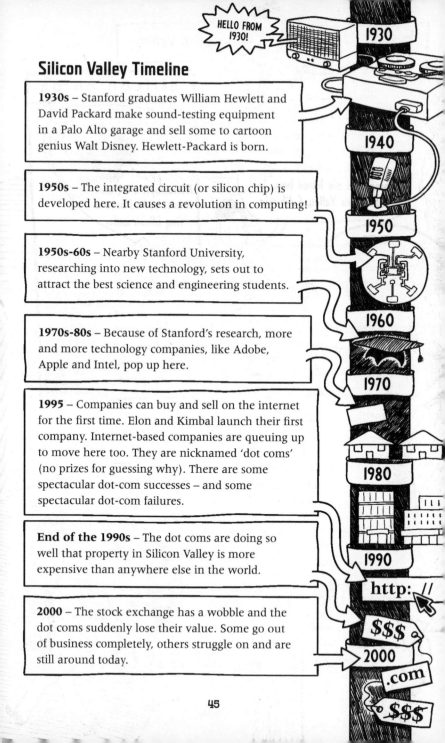

HELLO FROM 1930!

Silicon Valley Timeline

1930s – Stanford graduates William Hewlett and David Packard make sound-testing equipment in a Palo Alto garage and sell some to cartoon genius Walt Disney. Hewlett-Packard is born.

1950s – The integrated circuit (or silicon chip) is developed here. It causes a revolution in computing!

1950s-60s – Nearby Stanford University, researching into new technology, sets out to attract the best science and engineering students.

1970s-80s – Because of Stanford's research, more and more technology companies, like Adobe, Apple and Intel, pop up here.

1995 – Companies can buy and sell on the internet for the first time. Elon and Kimbal launch their first company. Internet-based companies are queuing up to move here too. They are nicknamed 'dot coms' (no prizes for guessing why). There are some spectacular dot-com successes – and some spectacular dot-com failures.

End of the 1990s – The dot coms are doing so well that property in Silicon Valley is more expensive than anywhere else in the world.

2000 – The stock exchange has a wobble and the dot coms suddenly lose their value. Some go out of business completely, others struggle on and are still around today.

1930
1940
1950
1960
1970
1980
1990
http://
$$$
2000
.com
$$$

Two's Company

Imagine a world where people go to the library if they need to find out the capital of Turkmenistan (FYI it's Ashgabat), or riffle through the pages of a thick telephone book if they want to order a pizza. That's how life was back in the 1990s, when Elon and Kimbal were having their brilliant internet ideas. Hardly anyone else could see how the internet might change everything, from taking and storing photos to organizing a party.

Elon and Kimbal's most brilliant idea was for an internet database you could search to find information, maps and directions for local businesses. They called it Global Link Information Network. The idea might sound obvious now, but back then **it was genius** and completely new. Unfortunately, not many businesses could see why they should waste their time creating anything fancy like a website. One company boss actually threw an old-fashioned telephone directory at the brothers . . .

You mean you think the internet will replace this?

Later, when it became obvious that Elon and Kimbal were absolutely right, the boss had to eat his words (if not the phone book) and he invested in the company after all.

Starting up wasn't easy, but the brothers had a massive piece of luck when their parents gave them money to help them get going. Elon and Kimbal rented an office in Palo Alto: it was tiny, there was no lift, and **the toilets kept getting blocked**. For the first three months, they literally lived at the office – sleeping on beanbags at night, showering at the local YMCA hostel, and working the rest of the time, fuelled by takeaways, Diet Coke and coffee.

> The programs aren't the only ones backing up around here!

After a few months, Elon and Kimbal were making enough money to afford to rent a two-bedroom flat, but Elon still slept on his office beanbag most of the time. Whoever got to the office first in the morning had the important task of giving him **a wake-up kick**.

The brothers were a good match. The more outgoing Kimbal had the tricky job of explaining the internet to local businesses, and trying to persuade them to join the database. He did it with charm and optimism . . .

. . . while Elon provided the technological genius and a determination to succeed. He worked feverishly on the software.

They got on pretty well, but if they disagreed about anything, they had an unusual but effective way of dealing with it.

By 1996, when more people knew about the internet and understood that you could make money out of it, the company looked **so impressive** that it attracted a huge $3-million investment – that was about **a hundred times the amount** Elon and Kimbal started the company with! They very sensibly changed the company's name from Global Link Information Network to Zip2 – the idea was that it helped people zip to one place from another, and it does sound a lot more . . . **zippy**!

Zip-a-dee-do-dah

Now things were really motoring. Zip2 began selling its business all over the United States, and employed brilliant engineers to make Elon's software even more brilliant. Elon was made chief of technology, while someone else ran the company. They moved out of their tiny office to a bigger and better one, with much nicer toilets.

Even better than the toilets, Elon and Kimbal were given **$30,000 each just to buy a car**. To give you an idea of how wonderful this was to Elon and Kimbal, their previous shared car looked like this:

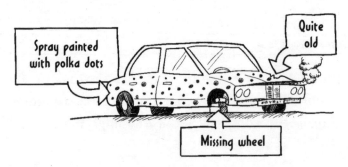

The brothers, and especially Elon, absolutely loved cars. It was a bit like two very sweet-toothed children being let loose in a sweet shop with unlimited money. Kimbal bought a fairly flash but mostly sensible new car, while **Elon chose his dream car**, a 'classic' 1967 E-type Jaguar. It looked amazing . . . but it kept breaking down. Elon regularly arrived at work in a flat-bed truck with his car on the back.

However, in the late 1990s, things at Zip2 were a bit up-and-down . . .

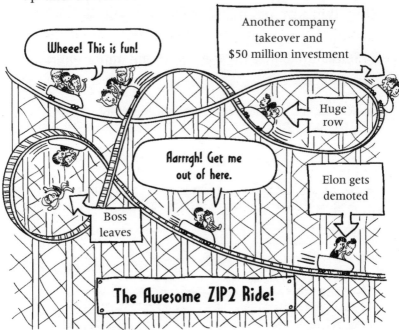

Another company takeover and $50 million investment

Wheee! This is fun!

Huge row

Aarrrgh! Get me out of here.

Elon gets demoted

Boss leaves

The Awesome ZIP2 Ride!

. . . until a computer manufacturer called Compaq offered a massive $307 million dollars to buy Zip2.

You might want to have a little lie down at this point, to get your head around the thought of all that dosh.

Kimbal got $15 million out of the deal and moved to New York City to take a course in French cookery (maybe it was all those takeaways). He loved cooking so much that he decided to open a restaurant.

Elon got $22 million dollars from the sale of Zip2. **He was now a dot-com millionaire** (see page 45) and he was still only twenty-seven years old. The question was, what was he going to do with all that lovely cash? He had absolutely no intention of putting his feet up and retiring.

First things first, though. Elon did allow himself a few luxuries:

- He bought a very flash apartment and moved into it with his girlfriend, Justine . . .

- And a propeller plane, which he learned to fly (like his grandad, Joshua) . . .

- And a McLaren F1, which was the fastest car in the world at the time and cost $1 million.

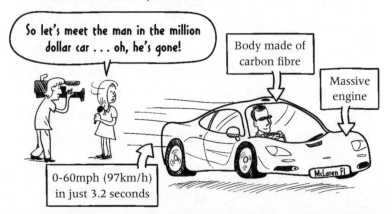

So let's meet the man in the million dollar car . . . oh, he's gone!

Body made of carbon fibre

Massive engine

0-60mph (97km/h) in just 3.2 seconds

McLaren F1

A TV crew really did film the delivery of the car for a programme about dot-com millionaires.

Elon loved his F1 and drove it everywhere, even to the supermarket. He kept it until 2007, by which time he was making cars of his own.

Wonga on the Web

The rest of Elon's cash went on a business idea that he'd had a while back. He'd even told one of his bosses about it when he was working in the summer holidays.

What if we could do all our banking on the internet?

Don't be ridiculous!

Back then most people weren't comfortable buying **a bunch of bananas** online, let alone trusting the internet to look after all their money. That was partly because internet security wasn't very good. Still, Elon was sure it could be done, and now he had some money to start a company, he had the perfect excuse to give it a go. Saving the world would have to wait for the time being.

Elon announced the start of his finance company, the mysterious-sounding X.com, a month after Zip2 was sold. **Things didn't go smoothly**: there were blazing rows, 24-hour working days, complicated negotiations, and more blazing rows, followed by Elon's co-investors stomping off in a huff. But eventually, in 1999, Elon opened the world's first online bank. By March the following year, X.com had more than **a million customers**.

Everything looked great . . . for a while. Then arguments within the company and competition from other banks meant that X.com began to lose money fast. Everyone lost confidence in Elon even faster.

Honeymoon and Hospital

But one person still trusted Elon. Justine. Awww.

But just as Elon and Justine were heading off to Australia on honeymoon, a group of X.com employees were plotting to get rid of Elon. By the time the happy couple arrived in Sydney, a new company boss had been appointed in Elon's place.

Of course, when he found out what had happened, Elon didn't feel anything like happy, and he got straight on the next plane to California to try and sort things out.

Most people would probably have stormed about shouting and calling everyone rude names at this point. But **Elon managed to stay calm**.

Although he was pretty cross at first, he accepted what had happened – even when the new boss had the cheek to change the company's name to PayPal. But he still really believed in online banking, and carried on advising the company and investing more money in it.

> Don't worry. I know what I'm doing.

Elon and Justine finally got their honeymoon in December 2000. They flew to Brazil, and then to South Africa, where they went on safari.

> This is wonderful.

> Yes. And what can possibly go wrong.

> Mmmm! tasty!

But something did go quite horribly wrong. Elon didn't realize it, but he'd been bitten by a malaria-carrying mosquito. Malaria is a horrible disease that's common in Africa, and can kill. Back in the US, it made Elon seriously ill, but at first no one knew what the problem was and he was **given the wrong treatment**. By the time Elon got the right medicine, he'd spent ten days in intensive care and come very close to death. It took him another six months to make a full recovery.

Elon had lost control of his own company, and **he'd very nearly died**! He needed a bit of cheering up. And in 2002 he got some very cheery news: the internet-auction company eBay wanted to buy PayPal, for 1.5 billion dollars!

See? Told you I knew what I was doing.

$1.5bn!

4 Elon on Mars

Of course, Elon didn't get to keep the whole $1.5 billion dollars himself. (That's a thousand times 1.5 million dollars, by the way.) But he did get an awful lot of money. After the sale of PayPal, he walked away with 180 million dollars – and it was burning a hole in his pocket.

Living a life of luxury wasn't at the top of Elon's list of priorities, and he hadn't forgotten about the whole saving-humanity idea. Silicon Valley and the internet were yesterday's news. Elon had something **even more interesting** on his mind. By now he'd moved to Los Angeles, and he'd started to look up.

Whoa!

Space Man

Not all that long ago – only two years before Elon was born, in fact – human beings set foot on the Moon for the first time. People all over the world watched the first Moon landing on television, and **their minds were blown**. Space travel was actually a reality! It had to be the start of something massive!

There were a few return visits, some space walks, the International Space Station was being built and things like that. But, in general, people weren't anywhere near as excited about exploring other worlds as Elon thought they should be.

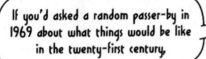

If you'd asked a random passer-by in 1969 about what things would be like in the twenty-first century,

they'd probably talk excitedly about bases on the Moon, and trips to Mars and even beyond.

It was a crushing disappointment to Elon that these sorts of thing had never happened. Everyone seemed to have lost interest.

What's wrong with people? Humans will need to colonize other planets one day because we won't be able to stay on planet Earth for ever. Some terrible catastrophe's bound to happen sooner or later.

Yikes!

Elon thinks Mars is our best bet, it's pretty close and in some ways fairly Earth-like – it has canyons, volcanoes, four seasons, a day on Mars is just over 24 hours long, and there are ice caps at its poles, which means Mars has water! In fact, some people think that – a very long time ago – Mars was a bit like Earth is now.

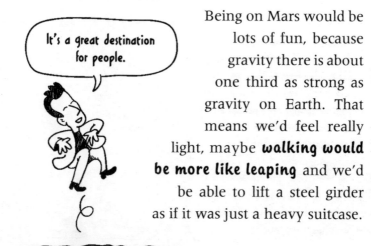

Being on Mars would be lots of fun, because gravity there is about one third as strong as gravity on Earth. That means we'd feel really light, maybe **walking would be more like leaping** and we'd be able to lift a steel girder as if it was just a heavy suitcase.

But we could live there without space suits if the planet was terraformed. Here's one way it could work:

At first, humans would live in a gigantic dome . . .

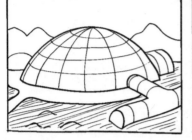

The ice caps would be partly melted, to release carbon dioxide that could trap heat from the Sun to warm the planet.

Humans could then grow plants that would release oxygen, and help Mars to become breathable. This would take centuries and centuries, but there might be ways of speeding it up.

By that time Mars could be transformed so it was more like Earth – except for the red soil and the two potato-shaped moons.

> That reminds me – spuds for tea?

Top physicist Stephen Hawking agrees with Elon.

> *We need to expand our horizons beyond planet Earth if we are to have a long-term future . . . spreading out into space, and to other stars, so a disaster on Earth would not mean the end of the human race.*

> If we can establish a Mars colony, we could go to the moons of Jupiter . . . and probably Titan, one of the moons of Saturn. The solar system awaits!

* This is an actual quote.

In one of his offices, Elon has two giant posters of Mars. One shows how it is today (i.e. red, dry and dusty), the other how he hopes it will be in the future (i.e. green and lush with forests and seas and things).

Thinking about Mars and rockets and stuff was **mind-bogglingly exciting**, but a few things had to happen before any *people* could actually get to Mars. Elon joined the Mars Society, whose super-brainy members all want a human settlement on Mars. They were planning to send mice into space, so they could study the effects of weaker gravity. But Elon had an even bigger idea – he wanted to **send mice all the way to Mars** and back, they'd even have babies while they were up there. Friends made a lot of jokes about cheese, but Elon was deadly serious. He desperately wanted to get everyone excited about space travel again.

Eventually, Elon started his own organization: the Life to Mars Foundation. He stopped talking about mice and began talking about plants. The plan now was to *start* life on Mars.

We can send a rocket to Mars with a space greenhouse!

The space greenhouse would land on Mars, open up, scoop in some Martian soil and plants would grow inside it with the help of a special gel. A video link to Earth would show viewers lush green plants growing against the background of the red planet. Watching a living thing from Earth growing on another planet – **now that did sound pretty amazing**. But how was Elon going to get his greenhouse anywhere near Mars when it would cost more money than even he had to pay NASA, or someone else with a rocket, to carry it there?

Greetings, Earthlings!

Right, that's it. I'll just have to buy my own rocket!

Actually, it is Rocket Science

The cheapest rocket Elon could buy back then was one designed to carry a weapon thousands of miles – an intercontinental ballistic missile. The Russians had some for sale, and Elon had just about enough money to buy one. He only wanted the rocket bit, not the weapon.

Most of his friends thought it was a totally crazy idea, and tried to talk him out of it, but Elon is the kind of person who designs Martian greenhouses, so off he went to Russia to try and strike a deal. His good friend, Adeo Ressi (from his party days back at Penn), went with him to make sure Elon **didn't completely lose his marbles**.

After three trips to Russia, Elon realized his plan wasn't going to work. Travelling home on the plane for the last time, Adeo was feeling miserable about the deal falling through. So was Elon, but not for long. He spent most of the flight working out how much a rocket would cost to build, and by the time the plane touched down, he'd already moved on.

Right, that's it. I'll just have to make my own rocket!

MASSIVELY COMPLICATED STUFF ABOUT ROCKETS

Elon got off the plane and went straight to work. He'd been studying rockets for months now and he'd learned an awful lot about them, but nowhere near enough to actually build one. So it's lucky he found someone who could – a brilliant engineer called Tom Mueller, who had built the largest liquid-fuel rocket ever made by an amateur. It was a bit like Elon's childhood experiments, but more complicated, much more expensive, and **slightly less dangerous**. Incredibly, Tom didn't think Elon's ideas were crazy.

And Elon realized something...

While all this had been going on, Elon had started a family. Justine gave birth to their first baby, Nevada Alexander, in 2002. But something terrible happened: Nevada died, aged just ten weeks old, while he was sleeping in his cot. Sometimes babies die in their cots for no reason that anyone can work out – it's known as Sudden Infant Death Syndrome, and it's incredibly sad, but it doesn't happen very often.

Two years after that terrible tragedy there was happier news: Justine had twin boys, Xavier (named after Professor Xavier from the X-Men!) and Griff. Always keen to do things efficiently, within a couple of years, **Elon and Justine had five sons**! The twins would be joined by triplets – Damian, Saxon and Kai – but not until a bit later in Elon's amazing story.

What's it like having Elon as a dad?

Well, the down side is that he's usually pretty busy, but there are plenty of up sides. The boys often visit their dad at work – in an actual rocket factory that sends actual rockets into space. They get to hang out with Justin Beiber, who's a friend of their dad's. There are holidays to the beautiful Hawaiian island of Maui, skiing trips to Aspen in Colorado's Rocky Mountains, and grandstand seats at the Monaco Grand Prix. Exactly – yawn. When they're not off on trips, Elon tries to get home early enough to have dinner with his family and just hang out doing ordinary dad stuff, like watching TV (except in a $17-million mansion in Bel Air, a very posh part of Los Angeles). Naturally, they play video games, but Elon insists the games have to be challenging – otherwise they're banned.

Some parents help out with the PTA or run a stall at the school fete. Instead, when Elon wasn't happy with the school his sons went to, **he started his own school** called Ad Astra ('to the stars' in Latin), in a multimillion-dollar mansion he bought just across the road from his own. Pupils don't have to stick to a curriculum – they're allowed to learn what interests them and they're encouraged to solve problems themselves instead of being told how things are done.

Come on, kids. You took it apart – now put it back together!

5 Elon Blasts Off

Elon invested a whopping great 100 million dollars in his new space exploration company.

SpaceX is Born

Elon really did think the whole project could fail. But he also thought that – with a bit of luck – it might actually make money. Countries and businesses already used rockets to send satellites into space for communication, weather, spying, navigation, research etc. If SpaceX could build one for a quarter of the current price, **everyone would want to use its rockets**, and they'd be bound to make money. So that was the plan: make space travel cheaper first, and save the important business of colonizing Mars for later. Simple!

SpaceX started life in an old warehouse in a suburb of Los Angeles. Elon celebrated the company launch in style – with a pair of maracas and a mariachi band.

Well, space is one thing there's plenty of!

The company's first rocket was to be called Falcon 1, after the *Star Wars* spaceship the Millennium Falcon.

Tom Mueller set to work building the two engines that would power the Falcon – they were called Merlin and Kestrel after other types of falcon, and nothing whatsoever to do with *Star Wars*.

The rocket was going to need months and months of testing, and Elon managed to find a site deep in the desert in faraway Texas, where **the only neighbours were cattle** – who wouldn't be able to complain about the regular explosions.

At the same time as the SpaceX team were working away on the rocket itself, Elon also had to consider the most pressing issue of all – money. **Each launch would cost millions of dollars.** While the tests were happening, and way before the Falcon 1 was ready for launch . . .

Good news everybody – we've got our first customer!

Whoohoo!

It's the United States Department of Defense!

Yeah!

We've promised them a launch date in 2004!

Eh! We'll never have it ready by then!

Well, come on, then – we've got a rocket to launch!

Elon was being a bit optimistic about launching the Falcon 1 so soon, since its main achievement so far was alarming cattle, and now the pressure really was on. Twelve-hour days and six-day weeks became normal for everyone working at the company. Except Elon – **he worked longer and harder than anyone**. But every so often they all took a break.

Even faced with a looming government deadline, Elon hadn't forgotten the importance of down time – especially if it involved video games. And if a good gaming session worked for him, why not the rest of his staff? At 8 p.m. he would often announce that it was playtime, and SpaceX employees would shut down their complicated rocket-designing software, and start up multiplayer, first-person shooter video games. Elon had always set aside plenty of time to practise over the years – back at Zip2, his video game team had taken part in national competitions and won second place. Elon's reactions were lightning fast and he knew all the tricks – so he often won.

With a lot of hard work, and a few breaks to have fun, SpaceX got their first rocket ready to launch in **super-quick time**. Okay, so their deadline was 2004, and they weren't ready until 2005, but that was only a year later than promised, which is pretty good timing in the world of space technology.

So what did the the Falcon 1 look like?

ELON EXPLAINS

Space Rockets

Rockets need oxygen to burn fuel, and there's no oxygen in space, so they have to carry some with them.

Rockets are the most exciting things on the planet by quite a long way. But they're pretty simple, really. A rocket contains giant fuel and oxygen tanks. The two substances are mixed together and burned to produce hot gases. These expand out of the rocket engine and push the rocket up and away.

When oxygen is a gas it takes up a lot of room . . .

but at −183°C it becomes a liquid, which takes up a lot less room, so rockets can carry a lot more of it.

Unfortunately the only way to fuel the rocket is by burning oil – specifically, a form of high-grade kerosene. Even I can't make a rocket that gets into space using solar electricity . . . yet.

ROCKET –
21m tall (the height of a seven-storey building) carries the payload into space.

FALCON 1

MERLIN ENGINE –
designed by Tom Mueller and mega-powerful.

It's ruined my marshmallow!

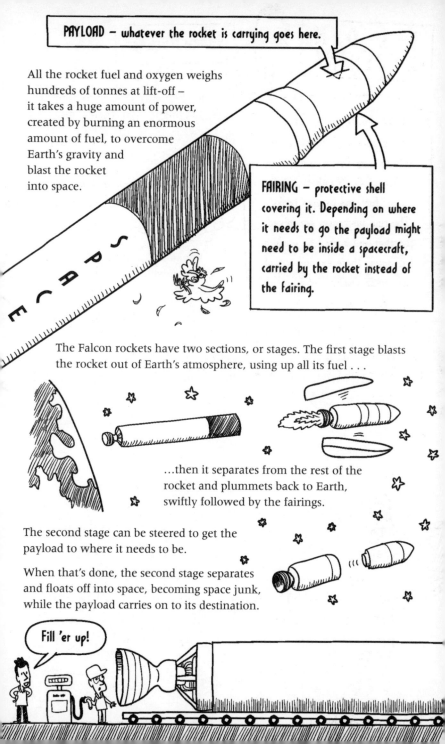

PAYLOAD – whatever the rocket is carrying goes here.

All the rocket fuel and oxygen weighs hundreds of tonnes at lift-off – it takes a huge amount of power, created by burning an enormous amount of fuel, to overcome Earth's gravity and blast the rocket into space.

FAIRING – protective shell covering it. Depending on where it needs to go the payload might need to be inside a spacecraft, carried by the rocket instead of the fairing.

The Falcon rockets have two sections, or stages. The first stage blasts the rocket out of Earth's atmosphere, using up all its fuel . . .

…then it separates from the rest of the rocket and plummets back to Earth, swiftly followed by the fairings.

The second stage can be steered to get the payload to where it needs to be.

When that's done, the second stage separates and floats off into space, becoming space junk, while the payload carries on to its destination.

Fill 'er up!

For its very first launch, the SpaceX team decided to use an old US-Army missile-testing site on Kwajalein Island in the Marshall Islands, in the Pacific Ocean. But once they got there, the problems started:

- The rocket fuel leaked
- There was bad weather
- There were issues with software ...
- ... and power systems
- ... and faulty valves ...

The launch was cancelled twice, and it wasn't until March 2006 – a delay of yet another year – that the rocket finally got off the ground.

The Falcon 1 took off like a firework, soaring high above the white sand and coral reefs of the island. Back on the ground, Elon and his launch team whooped, hollered, cheered and hugged each other. Hundreds of talented people had worked on the launch, it had cost millions of dollars, and finally it seemed that Elon's dream of space travel was about to come true.

The rocket looked to be on course. In just a few seconds it would leave Earth's atmosphere and head into space. But that's when things started to go horribly wrong. The rocket began rolling from side to side and **flames suddenly burst from its engine**, licking the walls of the craft. An instant later, Elon's worst fears were realized: The Falcon 1 exploded, sending clouds of smoke and flame billowing into the clear blue sky. Pieces of rocket began **plummeting back down to Earth**, crashing into the sea and spiralling onto the launch pad.

In the control room the cheering died down to a deathly hush. While Kimbal sat next to him, head in hands, Elon stayed calm. 'We'll get it right next time,' he said quietly. 'First time launches never work out.' Then he stood up and raised his voice to address the whole SpaceX team. 'Come on,' he told them. 'Let's find out what went wrong, and put it right.'

Almost as soon as the debris started hitting the ground, the engineers were trying to work out what had happened. The next day, SpaceX staff – some snorkelling, some diving – collected as many bits of wrecked rocket as they could find to try to piece the Falcon back together again. In the end, video footage showed exactly what had happened: it turned out the launch had failed because of a fuel leak . . . caused by **a single rusty nut**.

Launch Number Two

Another year, another launch. In March 2007, after rigorous checks for rust, a brand new Falcon 1 was ready to go . . .

The rocket soared into the sky.

The fairing successfully separated from the top of the rocket.

Everything was going according to plan, then . . . the rocket started to wobble.

The wobbling continued until the rocket began to break apart and seconds later, high up in the sky, it **exploded in a flash of orange and yellow**. The Falcon 1 crashed into the Pacific without reaching orbit. It didn't take long to diagnose the problem. Fuel sloshing about inside the rocket had caused the wobble and led to the engine catching fire.

But look on the bright side! For five whole minutes the rocket was doing fine. It really wasn't bad for a second attempt! And these are problems we can fix.

Although he sounded optimistic, Elon knew that SpaceX only had two more launch attempts at the most before he ran out of money. He stood to lose his whole investment, as well as his company, but he wasn't just worried for himself – the SpaceX employees would probably lose their jobs, **all 300 of them**.

Meanwhile, things were not going well in Elon's personal life either – he and Justine split up. As well as investing the last of his millions to stop SpaceX from failing, he also had enormous legal bills as the divorce was sorted out. Elon ended up having to borrow money from his rich pals – not just the odd tenner, but hundreds of thousands of dollars . . . every month! He even had to sell his beloved McLaren car (though he did make a profit of half a million dollars on it). Things were looking bleak. But Elon did his best to make sure the rest of the SpaceX team didn't realize how stressed he was. He stayed focused, worked hard, and encouraged everyone at SpaceX to do their best.

Launch Number Three

On Kwajalein Island, The Falcon 1 was ready for its third launch in August 2008. Engineers reckoned they'd sorted the fuel problem, and they'd even improved the engine. **Nothing could go wrong**. Tension was high as Elon watched via a video link in California.

The rocket blasted into the sky, shooting straight for orbit . . . but it didn't even make the first stage separation. Two minutes and 20 seconds after take-off, the first stage crashed into the second stage and the rocket exploded.

Not again! It seemed the new engines were to blame for the failure. The mood was miserable. Overworked and exhausted, some **SpaceX staff burst into tears**.

At this point, anyone might have been forgiven for saying something like, 'Let's call it a day. It was fun while it lasted, but this is never going to work!' Maybe that's what Elon was really thinking. But he certainly didn't say it. Instead, he said:

Elon's rousing speech had an incredible effect. In just a few moments, 300 employees went from despair . . .

. . . to hope!

Everyone worked harder than ever to make the next launch a success.

Launch Number Four (This Really is Absolutely the Last Chance . . .)

There wasn't enough money for a fifth attempt, so everything was at stake, on 28th September 2008, with launch number four. This time it *had* to work.

Elon was worried, of course. He was betting his fortune and 300 people's jobs on this launch attempt and there were millions of things that could go wrong. But, once again, he knew he was responsible for keeping all 300 members of staff motivated and so he kept his worries to himself.

He didn't want his kids to worry either, so he took them on a trip to Disneyland with their cousins and Uncle Kimbal. They rushed back to SpaceX's mission control trailer room to watch the 4 p.m. launch as it happened in the Pacific. The children were super-excited. Elon was excited too, but he was also **absolutely terrified**.

Isn't it great, kids? We're going to see the SpaceX rocket launch!

This is the most terrifying moment of my entire life!

Engineers at the launch site were exhausted; they'd been working round the clock. Staff watching the SpaceX screens felt **sick with nerves**. As Elon, Kimbal and the kids waited alongside them, everyone held their breath. Then they watched . . . as Falcon 1 blasted off and climbed up, up into the sky . . .

After 90 seconds, exactly as planned, the first stage fell away . . .

After three minutes, the fairing opened as planned, and plummeted back down to Earth . . .

Nine minutes after launching, travelling at a speed of 5,200 metres per second (18,720 kilometres per hour), the second stage reached orbit, and the engines shut down . . .

The launch was a success!

Back at SpaceX everyone went crackers. There were more tears, but there was dancing too, people hugged one another, cheered, shouted and laughed. And they had good reason: **this was the first time a privately built rocket had ever made it to orbit**. When Elon walked out of the control room and onto SpaceX's factory floor, an absolutely massive cheer went up. It had taken hundreds of SpaceX employees six years, and it had cost hundreds of millions of dollars, but Elon and his team had finally done it!

Either that was a successful launch, or I've just done the world's biggest fart!

6   Elon's Falcons and Dragons

While all that rocket building, blasting off and exploding was going on, Elon and the SpaceX team had also been making all kinds of exciting new plans, starting with . . . a much bigger, more powerful and absolutely enormous new rocket called Falcon 9.

Falcon 9 gets its name from its nine huge engines that are powerful enough to travel all the way to the International Space Station (ISS), around 400 kilometres above Earth. NASA had been using the Space Shuttle to travel to and from the ISS for 30 years and the old-style fleet of spacecraft was due for retirement. Elon was really keen for his new rocket to take its place – and **he wanted to make it reusable**, like the Space Shuttle.

If a cat can have nine lives, so can a Falcon!

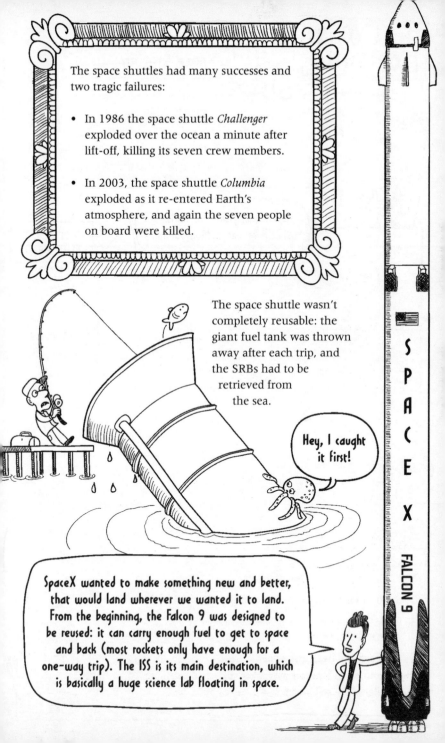

The space shuttles had many successes and two tragic failures:

- In 1986 the space shuttle *Challenger* exploded over the ocean a minute after lift-off, killing its seven crew members.

- In 2003, the space shuttle *Columbia* exploded as it re-entered Earth's atmosphere, and again the seven people on board were killed.

The space shuttle wasn't completely reusable: the giant fuel tank was thrown away after each trip, and the SRBs had to be retrieved from the sea.

Hey, I caught it first!

SpaceX wanted to make something new and better, that would land wherever we wanted it to land. From the beginning, the Falcon 9 was designed to be reused: it can carry enough fuel to get to space and back (most rockets only have enough for a one-way trip). The ISS is its main destination, which is basically a huge science lab floating in space.

S P A C E X

FALCON 9

ELON EXPLAINS

The International Space Station

It's the only lab where scientists can float about and really experiment with zero gravity.

Some nights you can even look up from Earth and see it without binoculars or a telescope.

• Like everything else in orbit, the ISS has to travel at just the right speed so it doesn't plummet back down to Earth or zoom off into space.

I told you we were lost!

• Only a lucky few become ISS astronauts. They have a strict schedule: nine hours of work (carrying out experiments) and up to two and a half hours of exercise every day!

THE STATS

• ISS took ten years to build and 16 countries worked together to make it happen.

• It's in orbit around the Earth between 330 and 410 km high.

• ISS takes just 90 minutes to travel right round Earth at a speed of 27,000km/h!

Did you put the cat out?

• Picture a six-bedroomed house whizzing through space – that's about the size of the ISS.

Two days before Christmas 2008, nearly three months after the first successful launch of Falcon 1, Elon got the best Christmas present ever. NASA gave SpaceX the contract for 12 flights to deliver cargo to the International Space Station using the Falcon 9. And they paid SpaceX **an unbelievable $1.6 BILLION**! Finally, the constant worry about funding was over. Elon cried with relief, then rushed out to the nearest shop to buy a Christmas present for his girlfriend.

The Fantastic Falcon 9

Falcon 9 is more than three times the height of Falcon 1, and its nine engines give it enough power to carry a 13-tonne load (Falcon 1 could only manage one tonne).

At this stage you're probably prepared for some more drama involving failed launch attempts and downhearted SpaceX employees, and Elon biting his fingernails but remaining positive for his staff. But that's not what happened at all. In 2010 Falcon 9 blasted off for the first time – without exploding – and orbited Earth. Since then it's been hard at work, dependably making deliveries in space like a rocket -powered Postman Pat. And at a cost of just $60 million a launch, **it's an absolute bargain**.

Incidentally, remember the mice Elon wanted to

send to Mars? One of Falcon 9's trips took 20 mice to the International Space Station so the astronauts there could carry out experiments on the effects of weightlessness. Elon finally put those mice into orbit after all.

Amazingly, and much to Elon's relief, Falcon 9's first eighteen launches were all successful. It was an incredible achievement, considering this was a completely new rocket. But then, in June 2015, a massive explosion destroyed the rocket and its payload (luckily no one was hurt). Elon got a horrible reminder of how easy it is for things to go spectacularly wrong when you're sending rockets into space: this time the disaster was down to a single faulty steel rod.

The Falcon 9 was designed to be reusable, but it wasn't fully reusable yet. At first SpaceX wanted to concentrate on getting it to do its job – delivering things to space – without worrying about the coming back to Earth bit. Because **landing a spacecraft is mind-bogglingly difficult**.

After getting to space in the first place – and we already know how hard that is – the rocket has to turn round, then burn a load more fuel to make the return journey, before landing absolutely accurately, without crashing – and all of this while the Earth is spinning and whooshing through space. Even Elon couldn't do that, could he?

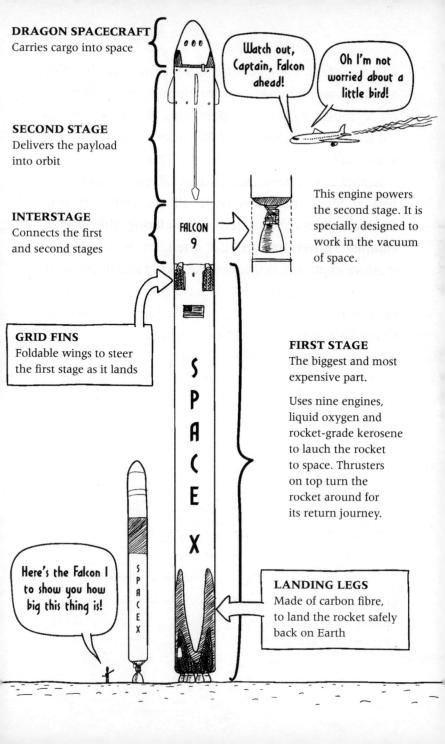

There were a few failed attempts, but in December 2015, Falcon 9 blasted off successfully, and while the second stage of the rocket boosted the payload into orbit, to deliver eleven satellites, the first stage turned round, plummeted back down to Earth, and landed safely and precisely on a target on the ground. No orbital rocket had ever managed to do this before. Elon and SpaceX had made **the world's first truly reusable rocket** and might just have reduced the cost of space flights by a third into the bargain.

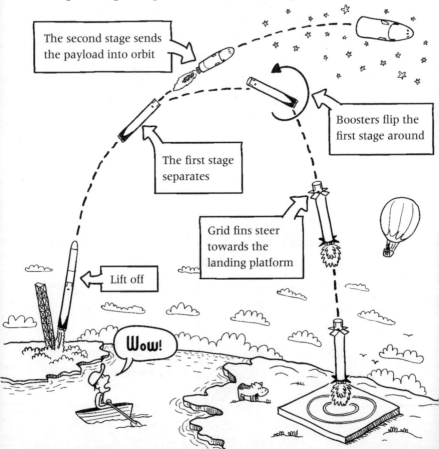

The second stage sends the payload into orbit

Boosters flip the first stage around

The first stage separates

Grid fins steer towards the landing platform

Lift off

Wow!

For Elon, though, there was an even bigger and far trickier world first still to achieve: landing a rocket on a platform at sea. Splash landing in the sea is relatively easy, but rockets don't like getting wet and salty (remember Falcon 1's rusty nut?). The tricky bit is landing on a platform, or drone ship. It's much more difficult than landing on solid ground, because, inconveniently, the sea keeps sloshing about, so the platform is always going to be a bit wobbly. On the other hand, there's a lot more sea than there is land, and landing a huge chunk of machinery at sea is far less dangerous to buildings and people. Elon and the SpaceX team were determined to do it.

The first two attempts to land Falcon 9 on a drone ship didn't go so well:

Landing 1: The Falcon bashed into the platform and exploded.
Landing 2: The Falcon landed so hard it broke two of its legs
and fell over . . . and then exploded.

Incidentally, the SpaceX drone ships are called **Just Read the Instructions** and **Of Course I Still Love You**, after planet-sized spaceships in science fiction novels by one of Elon's favourite writers, Iain M. Banks. The platforms were almost as complicated to build as the rockets.

Four months after its successful landing on solid ground, in April 2016, Falcon 9 delivered a satellite into orbit 35,000 kilometres above the Earth, then returned to Earth, burning through the atmosphere faster than a bullet, and **landed with pinpoint accuracy** on Of Course I Still Love You, floating in the Atlantic Ocean.

But making 35,000-kilometre-high deliveries in a massive rocket that could land on a floating sea platform was just a stepping stone for Elon.

A Solar-Powered Dragon

Back at SpaceX headquarters, the team was hard at work on a spacecraft that could fly on its own using solar power, once it's been rocketed into space. It was designed to carry cargo to the International Space Station first, but would eventually be able to take astronauts to the station too, and bring them back to Earth. Elon called it the Dragon capsule and, in 2012, it became the first commercial spacecraft ever to dock with the ISS. It's been ferrying supplies and experiments there and back ever since.

When a spacecraft splashes down into the sea on its return to Earth, the salty sea water can damage its delicate bits and pieces. SpaceX have been working hard to keep the capsule watertight, and on 3rd June 2017 the Falcon 9 took off from Kennedy Space Centre, with a re-used and refurbished Dragon capsule for the very first time. Elon's dream of reusable rockets and cheap space travel is getting closer all the time.

His mission to Mars is getting closer too, with the launch of the Falcon Heavy – **the most powerful working rocket in the world** – in 2018. It's the size of three Falcon 9s strapped together, which is unbelievably massive. The Falcon Heavy is designed to carry human passengers and could be the first Elon-made rocket that actually reaches the red planet.

Iron Elon

SpaceX is based at 1 Rocket Road, Hawthorne, Los Angeles, California, in a huge shiny white building with lots of glass walls. Inside it all **looks high tech and new**, and there are loads of people buzzing about looking important or excited, or sometimes both at the same time. But don't be shy – come in and have a look around.

Elon is quite fussy about the way his offices and factories look, and absolutely insists on shiny white walls and floors, even in the factory bit where the rockets are actually put together. The engineers, designers and sales people work in open-plan offices,

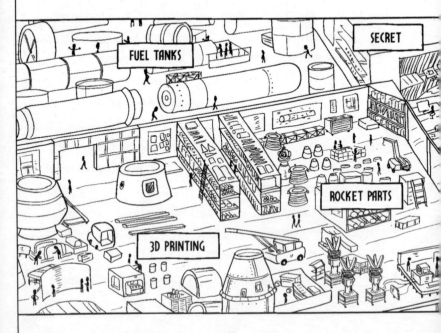

so that everyone can see what everyone else is doing. It could be the base for any company, except for the giant photos on the walls showing Falcon 1 blasting off from the Pacific-island launch pad, and the Dragon capsule docking with the ISS.

Pushing through the doors onto the factory floor you'll see **enormous great engines and bits of gigantic metal fuel tanks**. Cover your ears because the noise in here is deafening – most of the rocket parts are actually made on the premises. Hanging from the ceiling there's a real Dragon capsule that's been all the way to the ISS and back, and some seven-metre-tall Falcon landing legs.

Through glass windows you'll see the mission control centre, with rows of desks and computers and huge screens on the walls, for use when there's a launch happening. There's a clean room that you can't enter unless you're wearing a white coat and a hairnet – so that you don't contaminate any rocket parts. There are also some areas you definitely won't be allowed into at all, because **whatever's going on inside is top secret**.

Considering this is a rocket factory, you might be surprised to see a life-size figure of Iron Man standing by the lifts . . .

The only way is up . . .

Elon (aka Genius Boy): genius, billionaire, engineer and captain of industry who invents new rockets to save humanity.

Tony Stark (aka Iron Man): genius, billionaire, engineer and captain of industry who invents a powered suit of armour to escape his evil captors and becomes Iron Man.

You've got to admit, there are some strong similarities.

Robert Downey Junior, who plays Iron Man in the films, visited Elon in the SpaceX factory when he was looking for inspiration for the part. He wanted to **get inside the mind of a real genius billionaire**. Elon gave him a guided tour (of the building, not his mind) and some of *Iron Man 2* was actually filmed in the SpaceX headquarters – Elon even appeared as himself. In the film, he tells Tony Stark about an idea he has for an electric jet – it's an actual idea Elon really does want to work on.

Since then Elon's had roles in *The Simpsons* (in an episode called 'The Musk Who Fell to Earth'), *The Big Bang Theory*, and two Hollywood movies.

So, is Elon about to give up his plans for saving humanity for a career in acting? No, he isn't. He's got quite enough on his plate colonizing Mars, among other things . . .

7 Elon's Electric Cars

Way back in 1990, California needed to clean up its air quality and a law was passed that meant the largest car companies **had to make electric as well as petrol and diesel cars**. General Motors, one of the biggest car manufacturers in the world, began producing an electric car called the EV1. Unusually, customers couldn't actually buy the cars – they had to lease them from General Motors instead. Elon was still at university in Canada at the time, but he was very interested in what was going on.

Cough! Splutter!

Fantastic – someone's making electric cars.

Look, no emissions!

Then a few years later the law was changed, and electric cars weren't compulsory any more. General Motors decided their electric cars were too difficult to make, and they didn't bring in enough money. In 2002, because the EV1s had been leased and not sold, the company took them back and **crushed the lot** (there are just a few left in museums).

Some owners were so upset about losing their cars that they actually **held a candle-lit vigil** at the car crusher. How often do you see candle-lit vigils for things rather than people? These electric car fans were sending a very powerful message, and Elon was listening. He couldn't believe that General Motors didn't seem to get how passionate people were about electric cars.

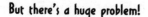

But there's a huge problem!

Why isn't everyone going electric?

If we carry on using fossil fuels:

- Planet Earth is going to get even more polluted.

COUGH!

- Greater levels of carbon dioxide in the atmosphere (see pages 34 – 35) will increase Earth's temperature and cause all sorts of problems.

- Supplies will run out.

Electric cars would be:

- Cheaper to run – electricity costs loads less than petrol.

- Easier to fuel – charging up overnight at home, like a mobile phone.

- Simpler to maintain – batteries powering electric motors don't have so many moving parts that can wear out or go wrong.

- Cleaner – needing a third as much fuel to run, cutting deaths from pollution and helping to fight climate change. Electricity is getting cleaner all the time too, as less is produced by burning coal and gas, and more and more comes from renewable sources.

If humans are going to have a future, there has to be a worldwide car revolution – electric cars are obviously the answer!

Surely, being superbusy with SpaceX and all those rockets and capsules and Mars and things, Elon couldn't possibly have found time for anything else, could he? Well, as a matter of fact, yes he could.

Electrifying Ideas

It turned out Elon wasn't the only person thinking about electric cars. A company called Tesla (named after electricity pioneer Nikola Tesla) wanted to make a sleek, fast, beautiful electric car, one people wouldn't be able to resist. Almost everybody thought they were mad – no one had managed to start a successful new car company in the US since 1925. But Elon didn't. In fact, he was so impressed **he put $6.5 million into Tesla** – more than anyone else – and became the company's chairman.

Elon devised a master plan for his automobile revolution and it came in three stages . . .

Master Plan Stage One

I've got a master plan!

The first stage was to make an expensive, flashy looking sports car, called the Roadster, to prove that electric cars can be super cool. As we've found out, Elon was a big fan of super-cool cars.

Okay, so the cars would cost a fortune and they wouldn't sell many of them but, Elon reckoned, if Tesla could make them just as fast and exciting as his beloved F1 McLaren, then electric cars would really get noticed.

It didn't take long. By the beginning of 2005 Elon was able to test drive a prototype.

By July 2006, the Roadster was ready to show to the world. It was a shiny, sleek two-seater convertible sports car, and **it looked amazing**. It was superfast too. An ordinary family car takes around ten seconds to go from zero to 60 miles per hour (97 kilometres per hour). The Roadster could do it in under four seconds!

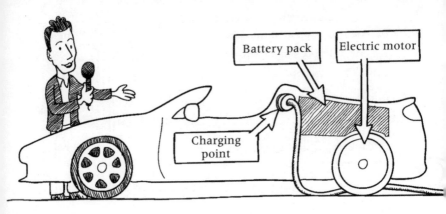

Battery pack

Electric motor

Charging point

Plenty of people agreed that it was a seriously cool car, and within two weeks of the launch event **127 Roadsters were reserved.** Anyone who bought one was given a certificate that read:

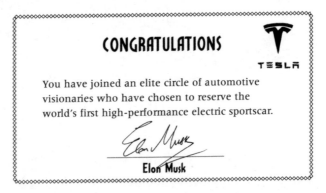

CONGRATULATIONS

TESLA

You have joined an elite circle of automotive visionaries who have chosen to reserve the world's first high-performance electric sportscar.

Elon Musk

People couldn't actually drive the certificate, though, and here's where things started to get tricky. They were told they'd have to wait a year, until summer 2007, for the car to be ready. Inside Tesla there were

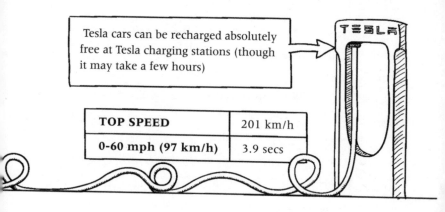

Tesla cars can be recharged absolutely free at Tesla charging stations (though it may take a few hours)

| TOP SPEED | 201 km/h |
| 0-60 mph (97 km/h) | 3.9 secs |

huge rows going on – some employees stormed out and never came back. Outside, some people were starting to turn against Tesla and the Roadster too.

TESLA – WHAT A LOAD OF RUBBISH!

TESLA DEATH WATCH
It's only a matter of time before Tesla goes out of business.

Electric cars? What nonsense! The Tesla Roadster sucks!

With his divorce going on, and those rockets that needed launching, it was round about now that Elon started running out of money. Generous friends invested in Tesla to help keep the company afloat, but they weren't sure they'd ever see their money again. Elon borrowed cash from SpaceX and anywhere else he could think of, but it was starting to look as though Tesla (and SpaceX too) might fail. Then, just in the nick of time, at the end of 2007, NASA gave SpaceX the lovely big Christmas present we heard about in the last chapter, and Elon had some funding at last. The day was saved!

Finally, in February 2008, Tesla delivered the first cars to its incredibly patient customers, and the very first one off the production line was claimed by Elon himself. Most people were happy to be driving a car that didn't burn fossil fuels and they could cope with a few glitches, but some weren't so happy: the actor George Clooney sold his Tesla after it broke down once too often (he'd already had problems with other electric cars). But overall the Roadster was a success. It proved that **electric cars could be fun to drive** and, best of all, that people really did want to own them. Over the next four years, around 2,500 Roadsters were sold, the car won awards, and the company made it to the next level.

Master Plan Stage Two

The next stage in Elon's plan involved selling a lower priced car to a larger number of people (it would still be very expensive, but you wouldn't have to be a billionaire to own one).

In 2009 Elon revealed the new Tesla. The Model S, a big luxury family car. Of course, it wasn't anywhere near ready, but it looked good, and customers **couldn't wait to buy it**. Though they would have to wait quite a long time to actually get their hands on it. Surprisingly, most of them didn't seem to mind.

The Model S won awards, not just for being the best electric car, but for the being best actual car – Consumer Reports organization gave it a score of **103 out of 100**! When they tested the car for reliability, however, they weren't quite so impressed, but that didn't put the public off. Tesla was soon doing very well indeed.

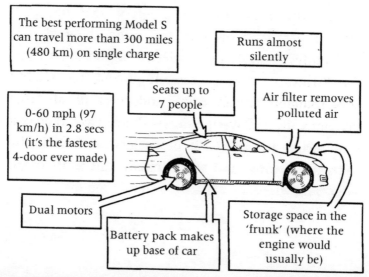

The best performing Model S can travel more than 300 miles (480 km) on single charge

Runs almost silently

Seats up to 7 people

Air filter removes polluted air

0-60 mph (97 km/h) in 2.8 secs (it's the fastest 4-door ever made)

Dual motors

Battery pack makes up base of car

Storage space in the 'frunk' (where the engine would usually be)

Master Plan Stage Three

Elon's final next stage would be to use the profits from stages one and two to develop a car lots of people can afford and make loads more of them.

The Model 3 was revealed in 2016, to a massive cheering crowd, and within 24 hours an incredible 115,000 cars had been reserved, though they weren't delivered until 2017.

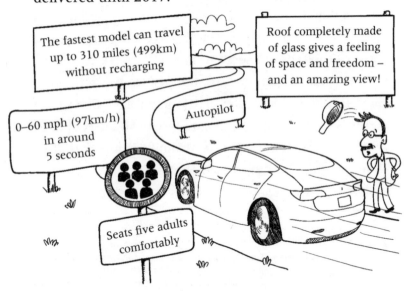

The fastest model can travel up to 310 miles (499km) without recharging

Roof completely made of glass gives a feeling of space and freedom – and an amazing view!

0–60 mph (97km/h) in around 5 seconds

Autopilot

Seats five adults comfortably

Eventually The Model 3 should help to make electric cars really popular, which is why Elon got involved in the first place. He thinks that **in 20 years' time most new cars will be electric**. So you never know, your family might own a Tesla some time soon.

Funny you should say that. Cars could be completely driverless in the very near future. The technology already works and it's being used right now in some places. It still needs a lot of safety testing, but by the time you're driving . . .

Yeah, I'll be able to get my driverless electric car to come to me!

I think cars people drive themselves will be a thing of the past before long. Some people might still want to drive for fun, just like some people ride horses for fun today.

Today, all cars have to have someone behind the wheel, but one day soon you really might be able to call your car from miles away and get it to come to you. Driverless cars might sound a bit spooky, but actually, **human drivers are far more deadly** – 23,000 people are killed in accidents on the world's roads every week, mostly when humans make mistakes.

Cars that can drive themselves could actually be up to 90 per cent safer!

And if all cars were driverless, traffic jams might become a thing of the past. Computer controls would mean cars could travel closer together because they wouldn't slow down and speed up as often as human-driven cars do.

Robot taxis are trialling in some US cities, and in California in 2017, 27 different companies were testing robot cars on the roads. All Tesla cars include driverless technology, and in November 2017, Elon revealed Tesla's electric truck that can be driverless too. It can travel 800 kilometres on one charge and carry loads weighing up to 36,000 kilograms!

Electric Inventions and Mega Factories

Most companies guard their inventions jealously – they don't want anyone else making money from ideas they've paid for. But Elon is so keen to make more cars electric (and not use fossil fuels, to cut pollution, etc.) that he doesn't mind whether the cars are made by Tesla or by other companies.

Go ahead – use the inventions! The more the merrier! I'm going to make lots more charging stations too, so no one needs to worry about running out of juice.

Yes, Elon's done something incredibly generous: he's made all the Tesla electric car inventions **free and open for anyone else to use**.

All these new electric cars will need an awful lot of special lithium-ion batteries and the world's current supply can't keep up. But – surprise! – Elon's already thought about that and he has a solution . . .

And, of course, the batteries can all be recycled.

Fun in the Sun

Every so often Elon needs more than a mega gaming binge to take his mind off the stress of his many responsibilities.

Along with tens of thousands of other people, he sometimes goes to an absolutely massive party that's held every year in the middle of the desert in Nevada. It's called the Burning Man festival, and it has lots of music, art, sculpture, spectacular structures that people set on fire (including, at the end of the festival, a giant wooden man), whacky-sounding events like 'monkey chanting workshops', and – look away now if you're squeamish – **a lot of naked adults**. Sorry about that.

Elon is still great friends with his cousins, the Rives from South Africa (remember the Easter eggs and the video arcade?), and they also moved to America. Back in 2004, Peter and Lyndon Rive went along to the Burning Man festival with Elon.

Elon hadn't changed his mind since secondary school – he still wanted the Sun's energy to power the world. Peter and Lyndon took his advice and, two years later, they started a solar panel company called

SolarCity. Elon is its biggest investor, and guess what? SolarCity has become a massive success. It's now one of the **biggest solar energy companies in the world**.

Hmm . . . an electric car company, and a company that makes solar-powered electricity – could they somehow work together? Well, as a matter of fact, they *are* working together. SolarCity makes the solar panels for Tesla's charging stations.

Working With a Genius

Now that we know a bit about Elon's companies, maybe you're thinking of applying for a job? Elon only wants the best, so you'll need to be absolutely brilliant and studying something relevant at college. Here's how he got some of the world's cleverest people to work for him. . .

Just as he did in the library as a boy, Elon can still soak up massive amounts of information and remember it all perfectly. So when you first start working with him, he'll want to find out everything you know. He'll expect you to work 16-hour days without flagging or making mistakes, come up with brilliant ideas, and find solutions to problems that seem completely impossible. And, by the way, **don't ever tell Elon that something's impossible**. He absolutely hates that.

If that sounds challenging and exciting to you, then you could be just the sort of person he's looking for. Working with Elon is no picnic, but most of his employees and ex-employees really appreciate the experience – even the ones he's fired – and talk about Elon like he really is a superhero.

8 What Elon Did Next

With five children, two enormous companies and a habit of working 80-hour weeks, Elon's days are pretty full. But his mind doesn't stop working as soon as he leaves the rocket factory. Would you believe **he's got loads more ideas** rolling around in his supersized brain? You're about to find out about just a few of them, but rest assured, there will be plenty more:

The Hyperloop

All those journeys between the SpaceX headquarters near Los Angeles and the Tesla factory near San Francisco got Elon thinking . . .

. . . and he had an idea. What if he built a massive

network of tubes just above ground and shot passengers along it? At the moment, it takes about an hour and a half to fly between Los Angeles and San Francisco. In this new form of transport the trip would be just thirty-five minutes. Sounds bonkers? Well, Elon made his idea public and now several companies are working on Hyperloop. One design looks a bit like this:

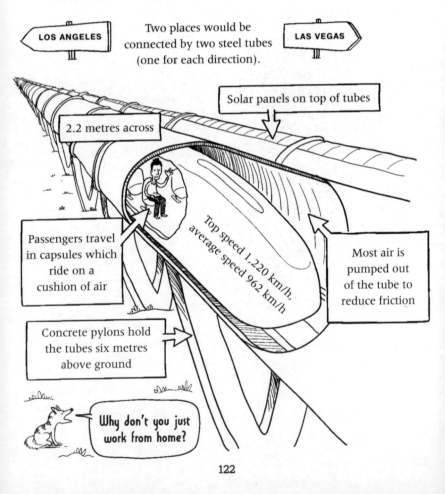

LOS ANGELES

Two places would be connected by two steel tubes (one for each direction).

LAS VEGAS

Solar panels on top of tubes

2.2 metres across

Top speed 1,220 km/h, average speed 962 km/h

Passengers travel in capsules which ride on a cushion of air

Most air is pumped out of the tube to reduce friction

Concrete pylons hold the tubes six metres above ground

Why don't you just work from home?

One of the companies is called Hyperloop Transportation Technologies (HTT) and they're already building an eight-kilometre section of the Hyperloop in California's Central Valley. They've started work on the world's first full-sized Hyperloop passenger capsule too. The company has even struck deals with countries from Europe to India to Indonesia, all keen to have their citizens travelling at astonishingly high speeds in the very near future.

Elon often finds himself in time-wasting traffic jams, so in 2016 he set up yet another company to help put a stop to them. The Boring Company isn't boring at all. Excitingly, its aim is to take road traffic underground on awesome electric skate pads, and zoom it along without annoying snarl-ups. Building (or boring) underground tunnels usually happens at a snail's pace – literally – and the Boring Company is working out how to make it much quicker, and much cheaper. The tunnelling technology will help to make Hyperloop a reality too.

Artificial Intelligence

Not to worry you or anything, but Elon thinks about artificial intelligence (AI) a lot, and he's pretty concerned about it. It's not human-like robots rising up and bashing people over the head that bothers him. Instead, think of **a giant invisible brain** with a will of its own, that has eyes and ears everywhere because it's connected to the internet, so it's also linked to all our cameras and other devices that are internet connected.

When machines get cleverer than us, they'll end up in charge.

There are thousands of brilliant human brains working on AI, but Elon thinks, if we're not careful, AI could threaten the whole human race! He's even invested in some AI companies, not to make money, but to keep an eye on what's happening.

Electric Planes

You can have electric cars, so why not electric planes as well? Elon is pretty sure that **all vehicles will become electric in the next 20 years** or so, planes included, and of course he wants that to happen as fast as possible. He doesn't have the time to work on it at the moment, so maybe someone else will do it first, which would be absolutely fine with Elon. Rockets can't be powered by electricity, but Elon does have some exciting ideas about **putting solar cells on the south pole of the Moon**, and making rocket fuel and launching rockets from there.

Submarine Cars

The 1977 film *The Spy Who Loved Me* made a big impression on Elon. In it, James Bond (played by Roger Moore) escapes from the baddies by driving his speeding car off a jetty straight into the sea. Miraculously, the car then turns into a submarine! Elon liked this idea so much that he bought the Lotus Esprit that was used in the film. He knew the Lotus couldn't really work underwater – the car was actually a shell and the underwater scenes were filmed with models, with the **air bubbles created by indigestion tablets**. But Elon wants to make a car that really does turn into a submarine when it's under water. This project is just for fun though. Elon would only make two or three because not many people would want to buy one. Who knows, though? How cool would it be to drive under water?

I think the market for submarine cars is quite small.

Is There Anybody Out There?

Here's something Elon is thinking very seriously about. **Have you ever wondered where all the aliens are?** The universe is very big. And it's been around for a very long time (over 13 billion years!). Life must have evolved on other planets, mustn't it? Surely we should be bumping into aliens all the time by now and real life should be much more like *Star Wars*?

> The fact that we don't know any aliens probably means that there have been lots of one-planet species that have died out. Let's try not to let humanity become another one. We need to get to other planets as fast as possible!

It seems a shame to spoil your day, but let's have a think about the terrible disasters that might wipe out humanity for ever. There have been plenty of them in the past:

- You've probably heard about the dinosaurs dying out 65 million years ago, long before human beings walked the planet. It's likely the extinction was caused by a massive great asteroid or comet crashing into the Earth.
- There were a few more extinction events before we

humans arrived, and the worst one killed 95 per cent of all living things on Earth. It's a miracle we evolved in the first place, really.

So, what might happen in the future? Well . . .

- After a nuclear war, Earth might become impossible for humans to live on.
- A terrible virus might wipe out everyone on the planet.
- There could be another massive asteroid strike. In which case:

We have two choices: stay on Earth for ever and be wiped out eventually, or become a multiplanetary species.

Which brings us back to Mars. SpaceX is already busy planning the Interplanetary Transport System (ITS), and it aims to start a colony on Mars with **one million people!** Of course, even though the transporter is the biggest, most powerful rocket ever made, a million people can't all fly up there in one go. It will take decades, loads of spacecraft and thousands of flights, but Elon reckons that a community can thrive with one million people, even if no one else rockets out to Mars to join them.

Here's Elon's plan:

1. To get the colony going, spacecraft land on Mars and leave major pieces of equipment to give the colonizers a head start – and they would need one! (For a reminder of conditions on Mars, see page 60.)

2. People start going to Mars in groups of a hundred on the ITS. These spacecraft will be reusable, and able to refuel in orbit and on Mars. But, at that rate, it will take 10,000 trips to carry one million people and the transporters will only be able to travel once every two years, when Earth and Mars are closest together.

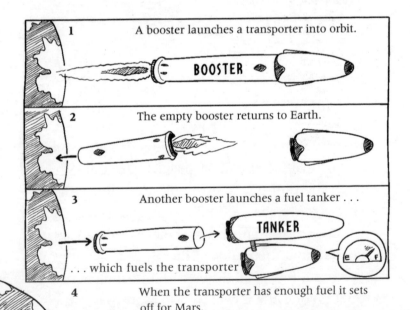

1   A booster launches a transporter into orbit.

BOOSTER

2   The empty booster returns to Earth.

3   Another booster launches a fuel tanker . . .

TANKER

. . . which fuels the transporter

4   When the transporter has enough fuel it sets off for Mars.

JOURNEY TIME: AT LEAST 4 MONTHS

3. So, eventually, bigger transporters may start carrying 200 or more passengers and there could be up to 1,000 spaceships in orbit – that could be loaded with fuel and cargo while they wait – to pick up passengers, like a kind of shuttle bus to Mars.

There you go – a colony on Mars. And in something like 40 to 100 years it should be growing food and feeding everybody who lives there. After that, who knows? People might travel even further into space and colonize more planets.

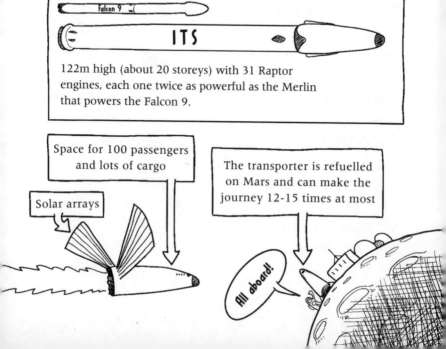

SIZE COMPARISON

Falcon 9

ITS

122m high (about 20 storeys) with 31 Raptor engines, each one twice as powerful as the Merlin that powers the Falcon 9.

Space for 100 passengers and lots of cargo

Solar arrays

The transporter is refuelled on Mars and can make the journey 12-15 times at most

All aboard!

Life on Mars?

Would you want to snap up one of those first tickets to Mars? And more to the point, have you got what it takes to get one? You'll need to be:

Adventurous and hardworking: The first passengers will have to find water and fuel under the surface of the planet – there's going to be an awful lot of digging to do. You'll probably have to build your own home too (which might be underground). Eventually, loads more skills will be needed.

Brave: There's no guarantee that every spaceship will make it all the way to Mars. Are you prepared to risk your life for a new world?

Rich: Elon has estimated that it will cost around $500,000 for the pleasure of the first few trips! He says the price will come down, though, so it'll only cost, oh, about as much as a small house on earth – peanuts really. The good news is that if you get homesick once you're there, you can come back again and the return flight will be absolutely free (hopefully you won't have sold your house to pay for the ticket)!

Elon reckons people will be queuing up to go, but he won't be taking one of those early flights himself. He needs to keep his feet firmly on Earth, to make sure that his incredibly complex plan runs smoothly.

But he has said he'd like to die on Mars – way off in the future, obviously, and preferably not by crashing into the planet in one of his own spaceships. So let's imagine what that flight might be like . . .

Some Time in the Future . . .

`Five . . . four . . . three . . . two . . . one . . .`

The countdown to the most nail-bitingly exciting moment of Elon Musk's life has begun.

Sitting in the Interplanetary Transport System is like being strapped into the biggest firework ever made. Elon spent decades of his life working to get it off the ground, and the spacecraft have completed the journey many, many times before – there are 250,000 people living on Mars now – but this is the first time he's ever left the ground inside one. It's the first time he's been into space, in fact. He's surrounded by friends and family members, including three of his grandchildren. The seats are roomy and comfy, but even Elon feels a bit jittery as they wait on the launch pad. So far the trips have run pretty smoothly, but you never know . . .

`. . .zero.´

The 31 engines fire. Elon's seat shudders and shakes as the rocket blasts into the sky. The journey now is the shortest it's ever been – just 30 days! The very first flights took nearly four times as long. Back then people couldn't believe humans would ever get to Mars – now spaceships are travelling much further.

The booster separates from the transporter and they're really on their way. The passengers relax, get up to stretch their legs and start exploring the ship.

While Elon heads to the lecture hall – he's giving a talk on his favourite subject, rocket science – his grandchildren have a game of zero-gravity football, which turns out to be even more fun than the regular kind. Some friends are heading off for a movie – they'll meet up with Elon in the Pizza Palace later. There's plenty of fun stuff to do on board – it's more like a cruise ship than an old-style spacecraft.

Just as he reaches the lecture hall, Elon turns to look through the window into the darkness of space, back towards a beautiful blue sphere hundreds of thousands of miles away: Earth – just one of the planets that human beings call home . . .

None of this has actually happened yet. Elon's grandchildren, and people living on Mars, are both way in the future. Even Elon can't be 100 per cent sure the whole Mars idea is going to work (and plenty of people say it never will). But then nobody thought Elon could make electric cars popular, or start a private space rocket company, or build reusable rockets that dock with the ISS . . .

SpaceX isn't the only company investigating Mars, but it does plan to send its first paying passengers into space very soon. And Elon reckons **the first humans could be travelling to Mars by around 2026**. Yes, he does have a habit of underestimating his timescales, but he also has a habit of making his own dreams come true.

The boy who built his own rockets in his back garden might well end up starting the first human colony on Mars – and ultimately **saving humanity**. That's what's so amazing about Elon – if things are important enough, he makes them happen even if they sound impossible. And he's got ideas about practically everything. Who knows what he'll come up with next!

Timeline

1957 Sputnik 1 is launched – the first ever satellite to orbit Earth.

1961 Yuri Gagarin becomes the first person in space.

1969 People walk on the surface of the Moon for the first time.

1971 Elon arrives on planet Earth – he's born in Pretoria, South Africa.

1983 Twelve-year-old Elon sells the code for his video game.

1988 Elon leaves South Africa for Canada.

1989 Elon starts college in Ontario, Canada, and the
years of studying and partying begin.

1992 Elon transfers to the University of Pennsylvania and lives in the
United States for the first time.

1994 Elon gets his first degree, in economics, and later a degree in physics.
The road trip with Kimbal happens this summer.

1995 Elon starts a degree course at Stanford
University but leaves after two days.
He starts Zip2 with Kimbal in Silicon Valley.

1999 Zip2 sells for $307 million – the brothers are millionaires!
Elon sets up the world's first online bank: X.com.

2000 X.com becomes PayPal.
Elon and Justine get married.
Elon gets malaria – and nearly dies!

2001 Elon moves to Los Angeles.

2002 eBay buys PayPal for 1.5 billion!
Elon starts SpaceX.
First child is born but also, sadly, dies.
General Motors scraps its electric cars,
Elon notices and has ideas of his own.

2004 Elon gets involved with Tesla and electric cars.
Justine gives birth to twins.

2006 Falcon 1 explodes on first launch.
Justine gives birth to triplets.
Elon gets involved in Solar City, his cousins' company.

2007 Falcon 1 explodes on second launch.

2008 Tesla Roadster is finally ready to drive.
Falcon 1 explodes on third launch.
On fourth launch, Falcon 1 succeeds – hurray!
SpaceX and Tesla both come close to running out
    of cash – but Elon saves the day (just!).
Elon and Justine divorce.

2010 Falcon 9's first launch is a success!

2012 The first customers get to drive the Tesla Model S.
Dragon makes its first successful delivery to ISS.

2013 Elon's Hyperloop idea starts to take shape.

2014 Elon enrolls his kids in a new school – his own, called Ad Astra.

2015 Falcon 9 reaches orbit and the first stage lands back on Earth
    – it's reusable!
Tesla Model X is delivered to customers.

2016 Elon starts the Boring Company, to move road traffic underground.

2017 Elon's gigafactory is up and running and producing batteries.
Customers drive away in the Tesla 3 – a more affordable electric car.
The first solar roof tiles are fitted to homes – and guaranteed for the
    life of the house!

2018 Launch of the Falcon Heavy – with a Tesla Roadster as its payload!

Coming soon...
Tesla trucks
The first passenger-carrying Hyperloop
Launch of the Interplanetary Transport System (ITS)...

Phew! I have been busy!

Glossary

artificial intelligence (AI)
A computer program that can think for itself rather than needing a human to tell it what to do.

asteroid
A small rocky body, much smaller than a planet, that travels around the Sun.

atmosphere
The envelope of gases that surround Earth (and other planets), held in place by gravity.

billion
A number that's a thousand times a million.

billionaire
Someone who has a billion or more pounds or dollars (lucky person!).

campus
The buildings and area occupied by a university.

captain of industry
Someone with an important job in an industry.

carbon dioxide
The main gas in the air we breathe out. It's also created by burning fossil fuels like coal, oil or natural gas.

carbon fibre
A thin, light material that is also very strong and often used in making the bodies of cars.

code (computer)
The technical writing that makes up a computer program.

co-investor
A person, or an organization, that shares an investment with other people or organizations.

combustion engine
An engine that creates power by burning fossil fuels, like petrol.

comet
A ball of dust and ice that travels through space due to the gravity of stars. When a comet gets close to a star, like our Sun, heat causes some of it to melt, creating a tail.

colonizing/Mars-colonizing
Sending people to a place (in this case Mars) to settle there to live.

colony
An area in a country (or on a planet!) under the control of a different country (or planet!).

contaminate
To get something dirty, dangerous or poisonous onto or into something clean.

dot com
A company whose business is carried out on the internet.

dot-com millionaire
Someone who has become a millionaire through a dot-com company.

dual motors
A car with a motor on both the front and the back wheels instead of just on the front wheels.

entrepreneur
A person who sets up a business or businesses.

fabled
Famous, especially because of their reputation.

fairing
The protective shell on a rocket that covers the payload.

forefather
A member of an earlier generation of a person's family.

gigafactory
'Giga' means billions: Tesla named their factory the Gigafactory because it produces billions of watts of energy.

girder, steel
A large beam used for building bridges or constructing tall buildings.

glider
An aircraft that doesn't have an engine, so it is pulled into the air by a plane with an engine, and then glides down to earth.

graduate
A person who has successfully finished their university degree.

gravity
The force that pulls people and things towards the centre of the Earth. All planets have gravity. Gravitational forces keep planets in orbit around the Sun.

hydrogen
A highly flammable gas that has no colour or smell.

hydrogen bomb
An extremely powerful bomb that is set off by an atomic reaction.

innovation
A new idea, product or way of doing something.

iron oxide
The chemical produced when iron is exposed to air, better known as 'rust'.

intercontinental ballistic missile
A missile that can carry bombs from one continent to another.

ISS – International Space Station

kerosene/rocket-grade kerosene
A rocket fuel produced from petroleum. It catches fire very easily!

km/h – kilometres per hour

lease/leased
To pay a certain amount of money to use something for a set period of time.

lumber
Wood sawn into logs or planks.

manufacturer
A company that produces goods for sale.

mariachi band
A traditional Mexican folk band.

microwave beam
An electromagnetic wave used in radar, communications and for heating in microwave ovens.

millennium
A time period of 1000 years.

mph – miles per hour

multiplanetary
On many planets.

NASA
The National Aeronautics and Space Administration in America. This is the US organization for sending people and robots into space.

nutritionist
A person who studies (or is an expert in) which foods are good for you, and what the food you eat does to your body.

orbital rocket
A rocket that can go around a planet, usually Earth.

orbiter
Spacecraft designed to orbit (go around) the Earth, while in space.

payload
Passengers and/or cargo transported by a space rocket.

photovoltaic cells
Cells that convert sunlight into electricity.

renewable energy
A source of energy that doesn't run out by being used, like water, wind or solar power.

solar energy
Energy from the Sun's rays. This can be turned into electricity through solar panels.

solid rocket booster
A large rocket that contains a lot of rocket fuel, used as extra power to launch the space shuttle. It came off the shuttle once it was empty, and fell back to earth.

stock exchange
A place where companies can sell shares in their business. Individuals and organizations who buy shares will get part of any profit, but may lose money if the company does badly.

sulphuric acid
A very dangerous acid that is used on Earth in factories. It will eat away at any natural materials.

telephone directory
A book listing the names, addresses and telephone numbers of the people in a particular area.

terraform
To transform a planet so it becomes more like earth, especially so it can support human life.

thruster
A small rocket engine that can change the course of a spacecraft in space.

vacuum
A space with absolutely nothing in it – not even air.

vigil
When you stay awake during the time you would usually sleep, especially to keep watch over something or pray.

zero gravity
The state in which there is no gravity holding something down.

Index

Use these pages for a quick reference!

A

Ad Astra (school) 67
aliens 126
army, South African 27–8
artificial intelligence (AI) 123–4

B

batteries, electric car 116
Bieber, Justin 9, 66
bullying 25–6
Burning Man festival 117

C

Canada 28, 29–33
carbon dioxide 34, 60, 61, 105
cars
   driverless 114–15
   electric 8, 39, 102–16
climate change 34, 41, 42
comics 16
Compaq 51
computer games 20–1, 39
computer programming 20
computers 20, 22, 33

D

divorce 80, 110
Downey, Robert Jr. 101
Dragon spacecraft 93
driverless cars 114–15
driverless truck 115

E

Easter eggs 12–13

eBay 56
electric cars 8, 39, 102–16, 133
electric planes 124–5
Elon's 50–1, 52–3, 81, 125
   submarine 125
   childhood 10–27
   children 66–7, 84, 121
extinctions 126–7

F

factory (SpaceX) 98–100
Falcon 1 70–86, 91, 95
Falcon 9 87, 89, 91–7
Falcon Heavy 97
family background 10–11, 14–15
fossil fuels 34–5, 42, 104–5, 110, 115

G

Gates, Bill 26
General Motors 102, 103
Global Link Information Network 46–50
gravity 59
greenhouses, space 62–65

H

Haldeman, Joshua 14, 15, 52
Haldeman, Wyn 14, 15
Hawking, Stephen 61
Hewlett-Packard 44, 45
honeymoon 54, 55
humanity, saving 8–9, 40–2, 43, 57, 58–9, 126–33, 134
Hyperloop 121–3

I

intercontinental ballistic
   missiles 63–4
International Space Station (ISS)
58, 87, 88, 89, 90, 91, 92, 133
internet 42, 45, 46–50
Interplanetary Transport System
   (ITS) 127–33
Iron Man 100–1

J

job opportunities 119–20

L

Life to Mars Foundation 62
Los Angeles 57, 67
lumber industry 30–2

M

malaria 56
Mars 9, 58, 59–63, 68, 69, 97,
127–33, 134
Merlin engine 70, 74
mice 8, 9, 62, 65, 91–2
millionaires, dot-com 52, 53
mobile phones 21, 22
Model 3 112
Model S 111
Moon landings 57–8
movies 101
Mueller, Tom 65, 70, 74
Musk, Damian 66
Musk, Errol 10, 19
Musk, Griff 66

Musk, Kai 15, 66
Musk, Kimbal 11, 12, 15, 19, 39,
43, 45, 46–52, 77, 84
Musk, Maye 10, 15, 19, 28, 39
Musk, Nevada Alexander 15, 66
Musk, Saxon 66
Musk, Tosca 11, 15, 39
Musk, Xavier 15, 66

N

NASA 63, 87, 91, 110

O

online banking 53, 54, 55

P

parties 37–8, 117
PayPal 55, 56, 57
Penn (University of
   Pennsylvania) 33, 36–7, 39, 40
planes 52, 124–5
pocket money 11, 12, 40
pollution 34, 35, 41, 105, 115

R

racism 10, 28
reading 16–17
Red Dragon 97
Ressi, Adeo 37, 64
Rive, Peter and Lyndon 15, 117–18
road trip 39–40
Roadster 106–10
robot cars 115
rocket

building 64–5, 68–86
buying 63–4
childhood 7, 18
Mars 127–9
reusable 88–97, 133
science 74–5, 93, 94
space 41–2, 64–5, 68–86
Russia 63–4

S

satellites 69, 94, 95
school days 25–7
Silicon Valley 38, 43, 44–5, 57
solar power 33–6, 42, 118–19
SolarCity 119
South Africa 10
space shuttle 87, 88, 89
space travel 57–8, 62, 65, 68–86,
   127–33
SpaceX 68–86, 87, 89, 91–7, 98–
   100, 101, 110, 133
Stanford University 43, 45
submarine cars 125

T

television 22, 101
Tesla 106–13, 115–16, 119
truck, driverless, 115

U

university years 32–3, 43

V

Venus 60
video games 23–4, 40, 67, 72–3

W

Wilson, Justine 32–3, 52, 55, 56,
66, 80

X

X.com 54–5

Z

Zip2 50–2, 73

So that's it, end of story... for now!

To keep up with all the new and exciting developments with Elon's rockets, cars and more, visit these websites:

http://www.spacex.com
http://www.tesla.com
http://www.boringcompany.com